The Mediterranean Diet Cookbook for Beginners 2022

120 Quick & Easy Mediterranean Recipes|

4-Weeks Flexible Meal Plan to Kickstart

Your New Healthy Lifestyle

Sarah W. Lee

Copyright© 2022 By Sarah W. Lee All Rights Reserved

This book is copyright protected. It is only for personal use. You cannot amend, distribute, sell, use, quote or paraphrase any part of the content within this book, without the consent of the author or publisher.

Under no circumstances will any blame or legal responsibility be held against the publisher, or author, for any damages, reparation, or monetary loss due to the information contained within this book, either directly or indirectly.

Disclaimer Notice:

Please note the information contained within this document is for educational and entertainment purposes only. All effort has been executed to present accurate, up to date, reliable, complete information. No warranties of any kind are declared or implied. Readers acknowledge that the author is not engaged in the rendering of legal, financial, medical or professional advice. The content within this book has been derived from various sources. Please consult a licensed professional before attempting any techniques outlined in this book.

By reading this document, the reader agrees that under no circumstances is the author responsible for any losses, direct or indirect, that are incurred as a result of the use of the information contained within this document, including, but not limited to, errors, omissions, or inaccuracies.

Table of Contents

Introduction 1
Chapter 1 Everything We Must Learn About The Mediterranean Diet 2
    What Is The Mediterranean Diet? 2
    The Potential Benefits of the Mediterranean Diet 2
    Mediterranean Diet Food Pyramid 3
    Mediterranean Diet Food List 4
    Importance of Olive Oil—The Core of The Mediterranean Diet 5
    7 Simple Ways to Start a Mediterranean Diet and Lifestyle 6
    Eating Out 8
    4- Weeks Meal Plan 10
    Broccoli Cheese Chicken,pg41 12
Chapter 2 Breakfasts 14
    1. Tiropita (Greek Cheese Pie) 14
    2. Savory Feta, Spinach, and Red Pepper Muffins 15
    3. Spinach and Mushroom Mini Quiche 16
    4. Broccoli-Mushroom Frittata 16
    5. Tomato, Basil & Parmesan Scrambled Eggs 17
    6. Mediterranean Breakfast Salad 18
    7. Red Pepper and Feta Frittata 18
    8. Spinach and Feta Frittata 19
    9. Greek Yogurt Parfait 20
    10. Power Peach Smoothie Bowl 20
    11. Amaranth Breakfast Bowl with Chocolate and Almonds 21
    12. Portobello Eggs Benedict 21
Chapter 3 Beef, Pork, and Lamb 22
    13. Roast Pork Tenderloin with Cherry-Balsamic Sauce 22
    14. Bulgur and Beef–Stuffed Peppers 23
    15. Beef, Mushroom, and Green Bean Soup 24
    16. Fajita Meatball Lettuce Wraps 25
    17. Spiced Lamb Stew with Fennel and Dates 26
    18. Lemon, Potato And Olive Baked Lamb With Pangrattato 27
    19. Zesty Grilled Flank Steak 27
    20. Pork Tenderloin with Chermoula Sauce 28
    21. Beef Kofta 29
    22. Spanish Meatballs 30
    23. Spicy Lamb Sirloin Chops 31
    24. Lamb Stew 31
    25. Seasoned Beef Kebabs 32
Chapter 4 Poultry 33
    26. Crispy Dill Chicken Strips 33
    27. Citrus and Spice Chicken 34
    28. Lemon-Basil Turkey Breasts 35

29. Chicken and Broccoli Casserole 35
30. Spinach and Feta Stuffed Chicken Breasts 36
31. Turkey Meatloaf 37
32. Chicken Pesto Pizzas 38
33. Chicken in Lemon and Herb Sauce 38
34. Tahini Chicken Rice Bowls 39
35. Classic Whole Chicken 40
36. Broccoli Cheese Chicken 41
37. Chicken Caprese Casserole 42
38. Moroccan-Spiced Chicken Thighs with Saffron Basmati Rice 42
39. Lemon and Paprika Herb-Marinated Chicken 43

Chapter 5 Fish and Seafood 44
40. Pecan-Crusted Catfish 44
41. Roasted Mediterranean Fish 45
42. Italian Breaded Prawns 45
43. Mediterranean Fish And Chorizo Stew 46
44. Baked Salmon with Lemon And Dill 47
45. Moroccan Braised Halibut with Cinnamon and Capers 47
46. Catfish in Creole Sauce 48
47. Asian Swordfish 49
48. Cod with Parsley Pistou 49
49. Seafood Paella 50
50. Grilled Salmon 51
51. Grilled Prawns Skewers with Zucchini And Bell Peppers 51
52. Citrus Mediterranean Salmon with Lemon Caper Sauce 52
53. Lemon Salmon with Dill 53

Chapter 6 Desserts 54
54. Cholesterol Caring Nut Clusters 54
55. Lemon Fool 55
56. Almond Cookies 56
57. Minty Cantaloupe Granita 56
58. Golden Coconut Cream Pops 57
59. Light and Lemony Olive Oil Cupcakes 57
60. Blueberry Panna Cotta 59
61. Cocoa and Coconut Banana Slices 59
62. Chocolate Hazelnut "Powerhouse" Truffles 60
63. Apple and Brown Rice Pudding 61
64. Strawberry-Pomegranate Molasses Sauce 62
65. Nut Butter Cup Fat Bomb 62
66. Creamy Rice Pudding 63
67. Greek Yogurt Chocolate "Mousse" with Berries 63

Chapter 7 Snacks and Appetizers 64
68. Roasted Chickpeas with Herbs and Spices 64
69. Lemon Prawns with Garlic Olive Oil 64

70. Mixed-Vegetable Caponata 65
71. Five-Ingredient Falafel with Garlic-Yogurt Sauce 66
72. Zucchini Feta Roulades 67
73. Parmesan French Fries 68
74. Stuffed Dates with Feta, Parmesan, and Pine Nuts 69
75. Mediterranean Scones 69
76. Pesto Cucumber Boats 70
77. Lemony Olives and Feta Medley 71
78. Bravas-Style Potatoes 71
79. Marinated Feta and Artichokes 72
80. Savory Mackerel & Goat'S Cheese "Paradox" Balls 73

Chapter 8 Beans and Grains 73
81. Tomato Rice 73
82. Couscous with Apricots 74
83. Three-Grain Pilaf 75
84. Garlic Shrimp with Quinoa 75
85. Mediterranean Lentils and Rice 76
86. Lentil and Zucchini Boats 77
87. Greek Chickpeas with Coriander and Sage 78
88. Giant Beans with Tomato and Parsley 79
89. Amaranth Salad 80
90. Puréed Red Lentil Soup 80
91. Lentil Pâté 81
92. White Beans with Garlic and Tomatoes 82
93. Mediterranean "Fried" Rice 83
94. Creamy Thyme Polenta 83
95. Greek Yogurt Corn Bread 84

Chapter 9 Vegetables and Sides 85
96. Spicy Grilled Veggie Pita 85
97. Baba Ghanoush 85
98. Artichoke & Olive Dip 86
99. Vibrant Green Beans 87
100. Couscous-Stuffed Eggplants 87
101. Spina ch and Sweet Pepper Poppers 88
102. Braised Eggplant and Tomatoes 89
103. Glazed Carrots 89
104. Sesame Carrots and Sugar Snap Peas 90
105. Sautéed Fava Beans with Olive Oil, Garlic, and Chiles 91
106. Roasted Cauliflower and Tomatoes 91
107. Parmesan-Thyme Butternut Squash 92
108 Lightened-Up Eggplant Parmigiana 92
109. Greek Fasolakia (Green Beans) 93

Chapter 10 Staples, Sauces, Dips, and Dressings 94
110. Berry and Honey Compote 94

111. Orange Dijon Dressing 94
112. Classic Basil Pesto 95
113. Citrus Vinaigrette 96
114. White Bean Hummus 96
115. Sweet Red Wine Vinaigrette 97
116. Maltese Sun-Dried Tomato and Mushroom Dressing 97
117. Vinaigrette 98
118. Tabil (Tunisian Five-Spice Blend) 98
119. Cider Yogurt Dressing 98
120. Apple Cider Dressing 99
121. Olive Tapenade 99
122. Riced Cauliflower 100

Appendix 1 Measurement Conversion Chart 101
Appendix 2 Measurement Conversion Chart 102

Introduction

It's true to say that we are what we eat! Once it comes to maintaining a healthy lifestyle, the primary focus is not on how much we eat but, ideally, the type of foods we consume. It's essential to make the right food and beverage choices to stay physically active. I spent quite some time looking for a healthy eating plan. Finally, I realized the Mediterranean diet is the go-to healthy eating option. It is rich in flavorful elements like fruits and heart-healthy fats and equally nutritious and delicious.

Currently, this diet is more popular than ever. Every month, I come across various publications documenting every portion of MedDiet. It is simple, straightforward, and unlike many other diets, it doesn't require eliminating fats but instead replaces the bad fats with good natural fats.

Since the Mediterranean diet reflects the traditional Mediterranean eating style, that doesn't mean we must travel to the region to discover their fresh food produce and delicious flavors. Instead, we have it all in our local markets!

I make every day the Mediterranean as this is a diet proven to come with a myriad of health benefits. For instance, it is known to reduce the risk of diabetes and cardiovascular diseases, thus, promoting longevity! Generally, there are no specific rules on how to keep the Mediterranean diet, but I usually follow the various established guidelines and incorporate the diet's principles into my daily lifestyle.

As we age, maintaining healthy eating habits keep us from developing conditions such as cancer, hypertension, and heart disease. Nutrition is among the best tools we have that help us reduce or prevent the risk of these chronic diseases. I am passionate about cooking and understand that it's easy to transform a not-so-healthy meal into a great-tasting and nutritious Mediterranean meal.

Also, I know that everyone understands the importance of a well-balanced diet, but very few tend to put it into practice. This book will clearly guide on what the Mediterranean diet is and what it constitutes, the associated potential health benefits, and various ways to start a Mediterranean-style eating habit. It will greatly assist in turning a day-by-day diet into a lifetime eating habit in a nourishing manner. If you are unsure where to begin, crack open this leading Mediterranean diet cookbook to get started on the right foot with exceptional recipes!

Chapter 1 Everything We Must Learn About The Mediterranean Diet

What Is The Mediterranean Diet?

Although the Mediterranean diet is typically not a specific meal, we can define it as a way of eating based on traditional cuisines that the people bordering the Mediterranean Sea used to eat. This includes countries like Italy, Greece, France, and Spain.

According to research, these foods made the people in the Mediterranean healthy with a very low risk of experiencing chronic conditions. The primary foods in the Mediterranean diet are plant-based, such as nuts, herbs, legumes, whole grains, fruits, and seeds. The main source of added fat in the Mediterranean diet is olive oil.

The Mediterranean diet can be used as a long-term dietary option to adopt due to its preventative health properties from the combination of anti-inflammatory and antioxidant foods. If you've ever visited the Mediterranean region, particularly Greece or Italy, recall the food you ate.

You likely consumed a lot of fresh produce, oils, and fats (like olive oil & avocado), whole grains (like pasta, rice, and bread), fish and other seafood, legumes, herbs, and spices. In addition, you might have occasionally eaten chicken, eggs, dairy products, and, even less frequently, red meat or something sweet.

The Potential Benefits of the Mediterranean Diet

The Mediterranean diet has constantly been voted the best diet. Despite being delicious and its numerous health benefits, the Mediterranean diet doesn't have food restrictions or rules, making it very easy to follow. It's a healthy eating pattern emphasizing healthy fats from natural ingredients and fresh produce cuisines.

Let's look at the various health benefits of this super diet:

✶Can Help With Weight Loss/Maintenance

This is a perfect diet for any person trying to cut some weight. Obese or overweight individuals tend to lose a lot of weight on the Mediterranean diet compared to those following regular low-fat diets. In addition, it is a healthy, safe, and sustainable way of losing weight since the natural ingredients included don't trigger extreme weight gain.

✻ Improves Heart Health

The Mediterranean diet has a significant ability to promote heart health, and research has linked this diet to reduced risks of stroke and heart disease in many studies. This diet has a high effect on slowing the development of plaque in arteries which is the primary risk factor for heart conditions. In addition to improving heart health, the Med diet has also been found to lower systolic and diastolic blood pressure levels.

✻ May Help Fight Cancer

The Mediterranean diet meal plan helps us prevent some forms of cancer. For example, it plays an integral role in reducing the risk of colorectal cancer, neck/head cancer, as well as breast cancer and preventing death among survivors of these fatal cancers. In addition, women who followed a Mediterranean diet with adequate amounts of extra virgin olive oil have had lower risks of breast cancer than those on low-fat diets.

✻ It Might Help You Live Longer.

When you reduce the risk of physical and mental health problems, you increase life expectancy by 20% at any age. Consequently, consuming nuts, whole grains, and legumes while limiting the intake of processed and red meats is the most effective method of increasing life expectancy. The ingredients in this diet have been associated with longevity, cognitive health, and better heart and brain health.

Mediterranean Diet Food Pyramid

The Mediterranean diet pyramid reflects the traditional lifestyle and dietary elements of the countries bordering the Mediterranean Sea. Therefore, this pyramid is used as a guide for the Mediterranean diet. At the base of the pyramid lies the foods you should eat daily and incorporate into everyday meals. They include veggies, fruits, whole grains, seeds, olive oil, nuts, and legumes.

The preceding tier lists foods you should eat at least twice a week. This includes fish and other seafood. Next are the foods to eat in moderation! These foods include cheese, poultry, yogurt, and eggs. The last and smallest tier of the Mediterranean diet pyramid includes some foods to limit, such as sweets, red meat, and saturated fats.

But what should you drink? Well, plain water with unsweetened beverages like tea or coffee is recommended. You can also take moderate amounts of red wine—just a glass during dinner! Other sweetened drinks like soda are considered sugary processed foods and don't have a crucial role in the Mediterranean diet.

Physical activity is also incorporated into the pyramid and the practice of sharing meals with other individuals to achieve a healthy lifestyle. It's crucial to incorporate these concepts since a diet will not cater to a lack of physical exercise. Although sharing and enjoying meals with others is a traditional way to connect, it helps build better relations with family and friends.

It makes a good sense for better health when we opt for the Mediterranean diet every month. Meals with exceptional flavor, affordable, and easy to prepare. According to the Mediterranean diet pyramid, the meals focus on good fats and plant-based ingredients.

Remember, the Mediterranean diet is flexible; some individuals choose to make it vegan or vegetarian, and others prefer the low-carb flavor by including fewer whole grains. So, you're in the Mediterranean eating style, provided you stick with the pyramid's principles; little or no red/processed meats and large portions of plant-based foods!

Mediterranean Diet Food List

A Mediterranean diet should highly contain healthy plant-based foods and relatively low amounts of animal products such as meat. In addition, the Mediterranean diet usually limits added sugars, refined grains, and highly processed foods. When adding canned vegetables or fruits, ensure you crosscheck the labels to avoid products with sodium and added sugars.

Water should be the priority beverage in the Mediterranean diet. Wine can also be taken but in small amounts. Sugar-sweetened beverages should be limited as they contain high levels of added sugar. You can include fruit juices in moderation but opting for the whole fruits is better to get the advantage of fiber.

The following is a list of the ideal foods to include or limit in the Mediterranean diet:

1.Foods to eat

The best foods to consume are those low in calories, added sugar, and sodium but have high levels of essential nutrients. Here is a selection of the healthy superfoods to add to your diet:
- Fruits-Choose fruits with skin and seeds, salads, and high-fiber fruits like peaches, apples, and berries.
- Vegetables-Cucumber, broccoli, cauliflower, tomatoes, and dark leafy greens
- Legumes- Dried and canned lentils and beans
- Healthy fats-Olives, fish, seeds, nuts, nut butter without added sugar, and avocado
- Whole grains-Brown rice, oats, bulgur, quinoa, whole wheat, and faro.

- Herbs and spices-Dried and fresh herbs

2. Foods to eat in moderation

The following foods must be taken in small amounts:
- Dairy-Cheese, kefir, and unsweetened yogurt
- Poultry-Eggs
- Red wine-One glass per day

3. Foods to limit

The foods to limit are those high in calories and low in essential nutrients like minerals and vitamins. They usually contain high levels of added sugar and sodium, which might cause severe health conditions and include the following:
- Meat-Red meat, lunch meats, processed meat, sausages, beef jerky, hot dogs, and deli meats
- Refined grains-Crackers, white pasta, chips, white bread, tortillas, etc.
- Refined oils-Cottonseed oil, hydrogenated oil, grape seed oil, soybean oil, and canola oil
- Added sugars-These are found in various foods, but the common include soda, baked foods, candies, syrup, ice cream, and table sugar.
- Highly processed foods-Granola bars, microwave popcorn, convenience meals, and fast foods.
- Trans fats-Fats found in fried foods, margarine, and other processed products.

Importance of Olive Oil—The Core of The Mediterranean Diet

Olive oil has a unique aroma and flavor—peppery, grassy flavor, and fruity scent that significantly affects Mediterranean cuisines. It is mainly used in salads, stews, fried foods, and desserts. In other cases, this oil is used for drizzling, dipping, and on top of cooked items to attain that grassy peppery taste.

However, when it comes to fat intake, the amount of fat you eat is not that important but the type of fat consumed. Bad fats are usually unsaturated and generally are found in animal sources. Conversely, good fats are unsaturated fats and present beneficial aspects to health. The perfect example is olive oil included in the Mediterranean diet. However, extra virgin olive oil is the best type! This oil contains essential components such as oleic acid and polyphenols that bring various health benefits.

Extra virgin oil is the main feature of the Mediterranean diet, which has been noted to have antibacterial characteristics that improve the endothelial functioning of young females. Consumption of olive oil has constantly been linked to lower cancer risks, especially colorectal cancer, prostate cancer, breast cancer, and fewer deaths arising from cancer. It exhibits epigenetic effect interplay that provides protection from cancers since it contains monounsaturated fats.

Due to the presence of antioxidants, olive oil has anti-inflammatory characteristics and provides numerous cardiovascular benefits. Olive oil and the Mediterranean diet have positive impacts on secondary prevention.

For example, in atrial fibrillation patients that underwent catheter ablation. The benefits extend to other multiple chronic conditions such as diabetes and cardiovascular diseases. This versatile oil helps control insulin levels, lowers blood pressure, and improves blood lipid levels.

7 Simple Ways to Start a Mediterranean Diet and Lifestyle

The Mediterranean diet is so appealing that it has been named the best diet of the year four times consecutively. Everybody can follow the MedDiet.
So, if you plan to venture into the Mediterranean lifestyle, you must shop for delectable ingredients with an iconically healthy and delicious meal plan featuring the outstanding olive oil.

The Med diet, modeled after the traditional eating ideas of the Greeks and Italians, isn't typically more of a diet but an eating style.

Slowly introducing med diet foods into your meal is a great start, and then commit over time. Practical transition tips help focus on the diet by presenting simple techniques guiding what to eat and how to eat it!

Here are some of the simple ways to start a Mediterranean lifestyle:

1.Eat Breakfast Every Day, No Matter How Busy You Are!

It's good to begin your day with a healthy meal. A breakfast meal with balanced portions of whole grains, fruits, and some vegetables is the recommended step to begin your day. Good options for breakfast include a whole-grain pancake and fresh berries plus yogurt, a vegetable omelet and frittata, or a breakfast wrap. We all understand that breakfast is the most important meal of the day since it keeps you energized and productive throughout the day and reduces the chances of obesity.

2.Understand the Difference Between Healthy Fats And Unhealthy Fats

Include healthy fat sources in your diet on a regular basis, particularly extra-virgin olive oil, almonds, sunflower seeds, peanuts, olives, and avocados. The main source of additional fat in the MedDiet is olive oil. Low-density lipoproteins or "bad" cholesterol and total cholesterol are decreased by the monounsaturated fats found in olive oil.

The monounsaturated fat is also present in nuts and seeds. Omega-3 fatty acids and antioxidants are found in plant-based fats, including extra virgin olive oil, avocados, and seeds.

Unhealthy or saturated fats are mostly found in animal products. Consuming trans fats and saturated fats in excess can increase your risk of diseases and raise your cholesterol levels, so limit your intake of these types of fats.

3.Pack In As Many Vegetables Into Your Meals

One of the critical components of the Med diet is its high vegetable content. Therefore, your meals should primarily consist of vegetables. Although the Mediterranean diet recommends 7-10 servings of fruits/vegetables daily, studies have shown that even 3-5 servings can lower the risk of heart disease.

Vegetables like green beans, peas, eggplant, artichokes, and okra should be cooked in olive oil, herbs, and tomato to achieve that, and they are served with feta cheese and bread. Consider simple changes to your diet to include more veggies, such as introducing spinach to your eggs, piling avocado and cucumber on your sandwich, and replacing crackers with apples and nut butter for snacks.

4.Reduce Your Meat Intake

Red and processed meats should be rarely consumed. You can limit eating red meat to special occasions. The Mediterranean diet emphasizes a minimal amount of meat consumption. We don't require that much meat, and analyses have shown that limiting meat intake is linked to improved health.
You can try the following recommendations: red meat, poultry, and fish once a week. We're not advocating against meat, but reducing the saturated and trans fats in animal products may benefit your health.

5.Eat Seafood Twice A Week.

Every cell in the human body needs protein to stay healthy; protein aids in developing, preserving, and regenerating body tissues. The Med diet provides small to moderate portions of marine and animal-based proteins in addition to the plant-based proteins found in whole grains, legumes, and vegetables.
The primary protein sources in the Med diet are fatty fish like tuna, salmon, mackerel, and herring. High quantities of omega-3 fatty acids found in these fish help lower inflammation and raise cholesterol levels. Although not as abundant in omega-3s, white fish and shellfish are still excellent sources of lean protein.

6.Make It A Goal To Sit Down At The Family Table For Dinner Consistently.

Regular family dinners are tough for many of us to enjoy because of our busy schedules, but they are still vital for our health and our children's health. In addition, the majority of cultures perceive eating as a pleasant activity best enjoyed with loved ones and friends while savoring well-prepared, wholesome foods and beverages.

"Walking with family and friends is part of the Mediterranean lifestyle." In a typical Mediterranean home, sharing meals with friends and family is expected. This prolongs the time spent eating by enabling a discussion to be carried on during the meal.

Enjoy as many meals as you can with others. This is beneficial to your lifestyle in multiple ways. Our moods improve, and our stress levels drop when we spend time with our loved ones. However, being deliberate and taking our time to interact with others allows us to manage our portions.

7.Get Moving

Physical exercises are critical in maintaining a healthy lifestyle. Walks are one of the fundamental physical activities to keep you fit. It's crucial to spend more time moving about rather than sitting down.

There is a noticeable increase in physical activity with each step. You can also join dancing classes, go for bicycle rides, do hikes, do yoga, go to the gym, or go for a run. Ideally, set some 30 minutes for exercise daily and focus on committing yourself over time.

Eating Out

Since the Mediterranean diet highly focuses on plant foods, the selected ingredients should be cooked with flavorful spices and healthful fats—Olive Oil. It won't be surprising to find out that many Mediterranean foods are our daily favorites.

There are numerous eateries with meals that fit into the Mediterranean diet. However, you should primarily focus on healthy fats, legumes, whole grains, and seafood. Then, create the perfect combination and share it with family or friends for an outstanding dining experience.

If you love the Mediterranean diet, here are some excellent tips for adapting your cuisines when eating out:

1.Order a whole grain meal with the largest proportion on your plate

2.Complement with some vegetables

3.Request if your meal can be prepared with extra virgin oil instead of butter

4. Add some fish or delectable seafood to your order

5. Order a glass of red wine

Following the Mediterranean diet entails making some sustainable and long-term dietary changes. These changes affect and improve your way of eating within a month and for the rest of your life. It's always recommended that your diet be rich in natural foods with plenty of vegetables, fruits, healthy fats, and whole grains.

Shopping at the store's outer edges, where the whole foods are often placed, is often a good idea. Choose foods high in nutrients whenever possible, such as apples, greens, peanuts, legumes, and whole grains.

Though there is no specific meal for the Mediterranean diet, its dietary combination is excellent with fewer animal foods and large portions of plant foods. The best part is that this diet's principles can be adapted in a way suitable for everyone. So whether you like seafood, olive oil, or vegetables, you can efficiently start building a delicious Mediterranean-style meal with the ingredients you love!

4-Weeks Meal Plan

Week 1

	Breakfast	Lunch	Dinner	Desserts
Monday	Tiropita (Greek Cheese Pie),pg14	Pecan-Crusted Catfish,pg44	Roast Pork Tenderloin with Cherry-Balsamic Sauce,pg22	Cholesterol Caring Nut Clusters,pg54
Tuesday	Savory Feta, Spinach, and Red Pepper Muffins,pg15	Bulgur and Beef–Stuffed Peppers,pg23	Giant Beans with Tomato and Parsley,pg79	Lemon Fool, Pg55
Wednesday	Spinach and Mushroom Mini Quiche,pg16	Catfish in Creole Sauce,pg48	Beef, Mushroom, and Green Bean Soup,pg24	Almond Cookies, Pg56
Thursday	Broccoli-Mushroom Frittata,pg16	Lemon, Potato And Olive Baked Lamb With Pangrattato,pg27	Roasted Mediterranean Fish,Pg45	Minty Cantaloupe Granita, pg56
Friday	Tomato, Basil & Parmesan Scrambled Eggs, pg17	Moroccan-Spiced Chicken Thighs with Saffron Basmati Rice,pg42	Spiced Lamb Stew with Fennel and Dates,pg26	Golden Coconut Cream Pops, pg57
Saturday	Spinach and Feta Frittata,pg19	Tomato Rice, Pg73	Classic Whole Chicken,pg40	Light and Lemony Olive Oil Cupcakes, pg57
Sunday	Zucchini Feta Roulades, pg67	Parmesan French Fries,pg68	Asian Swordfish, pg49	Blueberry Panna Cotta,pg59

Week 2

	Breakfast	Lunch	Dinner	Desserts
Monday	Couscous with Apricots, pg74	Lemon, Potato And Olive Baked Lamb With Pangrattato, pg27	Puréed Red Lentil Soup, pg80	Mediterranean Scones, pg69
Tuesday	Greek Yogurt Parfait, pg20	Bravas-Style Potatoes, pg71	Pork Tenderloin with Chermoula Sauce, pg28	Chocolate Hazelnut "Powerhouse" Truffles, pg60
Wednesday	Power Peach Smoothie Bowl, pg20	Mediterranean Fish And Chorizo Stew, Pg46	Citrus and Spice Chicken, pg34	Apple and Brown Rice Pudding, pg61
Thursday	Amaranth Breakfast Bowl with Chocolate and Almonds, pg21	Lentil and Zucchini Boats, pg77	Spanish Meatballs, Pg30	Strawberry-Pomegranate Molasses Sauce, pg62
Friday	Creamy Thyme Polenta, pg83	Cod with Parsley Pistou, pg49	Spicy Lamb Sirloin Chops, pg31	Nut Butter Cup Fat Bomb, pg62
Saturday	Five-Ingredient Falafel with Garlic-Yogurt Sauce, pg66	Moroccan-Spiced Chicken Thighs with Saffron Basmati Rice, pg42	Lemon-Basil Turkey Breasts, pg35	Greek Yogurt Chocolate "Mousse" with Berries, pg63
Sunday	Mixed-Vegetable Caponata, pg65	Baba Ghanoush, Pg85	Lemon and Paprika Herb-Marinated Chicken, pg43	Creamy Rice Pudding, pg63

Week 3

	Breakfast	Lunch	Dinner	Desserts
Monday	Red Pepper and Feta Frittata, pg18	Lemon Prawns with Garlic Olive Oill,pg64	Mediterranean "Fried" Rice, Pg83	Stuffed Dates with Feta, Parmesan, and Pine Nuts,pg69
Tuesday	White Bean Hummus, pg96	Roasted Cauliflower and Tomatoes, Pg91	Lamb Stew, Pg31	Marinated Feta and Artichokes, pg72
Wednesday	Mediterranean Breakfast Salad, pg18	Baked Salmon with Lemon And Dill ,pg47	Broccoli Cheese Chicken,pg41	Cocoa and Coconut Banana Slices,pg59
Thursday	Lemony Olives and Feta Medley,pg71	Couscous-Stuffed Eggplants,pg87	Chicken in Lemon and Herb Sauce,pg38	Spina ch and Sweet Pepper Poppers,pg88
Friday	Three-Grain Pilaf,pg75	Garlic Shrimp with Quinoa, Pg75	Mediterranean Lentils and Rice,pg76	Savory Mackerel & Goat'S Cheese "Paradox" Balls,pg73
Saturday	Amaranth Salad,pg80	Grilled Salmon, pg51	Beef Kofta,pg29	Pesto Cucumber Boats,pg70
Sunday	Creamy Thyme Polenta,pg83	Chicken and Broccoli Casserole,pg35	Moroccan Braised Halibut with Cinnamon and Capers,pg47	Greek Yogurt Corn Bread, Pg84

Week 4

	Breakfast	Lunch	Dinner	Desserts
Monday	Lentil Pâté, Pg81	Greek Chickpeas with Coriander and Sage, pg78	Spinach and Feta Stuffed Chicken Breasts, pg36	Parmesan-Thyme Butternut Squash, pg92
Tuesday	Portobello Eggs Benedict, pg21	Chicken Pesto Pizzas, pg38	Grilled Prawns Skewers with Zucchini And Bell Peppers, pg51	Glazed Carrots, Pg89
Wednesday	Pesto Cucumber Boats, pg70	Artichoke & Olive Dip, pg86	Seasoned Beef Kebabs, pg32	Berry and Honey Compote, pg94
Thursday	Spicy Grilled Veggie Pita, Pg85	Seafood Paella, Pg50	Turkey Meatloaf, pg37	Sesame Carrots and Sugar Snap Peas, pg90
Friday	Italian Breaded Prawns, pg45	Chicken Caprese Casserole, pg42	Braised Eggplant and Tomatoes, Pg89	Lemony Olives and Feta Medley, pg71
Saturday	Riced Cauliflower, pg100	Citrus Mediterranean Salmon with Lemon Caper Sauce, pg52	Zesty Grilled Flank Steak, Pg27	Roasted Chickpeas with Herbs and Spices, pg64
Sunday	Greek Fasolakia (Green Beans), Pg94	Vibrant Green Beans, pg87	Tahini Chicken Rice Bowls, pg39	Cider Yogurt Dressing, pg99

Chapter 2 Breakfasts

1. Tiropita (Greek Cheese Pie)

Prep time: 15 minutes | Cook time: 45 minutes | Serves 12

15ml extra virgin olive oil plus 45ml for brushing

454g crumbled feta

227g ricotta cheese

6g chopped fresh mint, or 3g dried mint

6g chopped fresh dill, or 3g dried dill

0.5g freshly ground black pepper

3 eggs

12 filo sheets, defrosted

3g white sesame seeds

Preheat the oven to 350°F (180 C). Brush a 9 × 13-inch (23 × 33cm) casserole dish with olive oil.

1. Combine the feta and ricotta in a large bowl, using a fork to mash the ingredients together. Add the mint, dill, and black pepper, and mix well. In a small bowl, beat the eggs and then add them to the cheese mixture along with 15ml olive oil. Mix well.
2. Carefully place 1 phyllo sheet in the bottom of the prepared dish. (Keep the rest of the dough covered with a damp towel.) Brush the sheet with olive oil, then place a second phyllo sheet on top of the first and brush with olive oil. Repeat until you have 6 layers of phyllo.
3. Spread the cheese mixture evenly over the phyllo and then fold the excess phyllo edges in and over the mixture.
4. Cover the mixture with 6 more phyllo sheets, repeating the process by placing a single phyllo sheet in the pan and brushing it with olive oil. Roll the excess phyllo in to form an edge around the pie.
5. Brush the top phyllo layer with olive oil and then use a sharp knife to score it into 12 pieces, being careful to cut only through the first 3–4 layers of the phyllo dough. Sprinkle the sesame seeds and a bit of water over the top of the pie.
6. Place the pie on the middle rack of the oven. Bake for 40 minutes or until the phyllo turns a deep golden color. Carefully lift one side of the pie to ensure

the bottom crust is baked. If it's baked, move the pan to the bottom rack and bake for an additional 5 minutes.

7. Remove the pie from the oven and set aside to cool for 15 minutes. Use a sharp knife to cut the pie into 12 pieces. Store covered in the refrigerator for up to 3 days.

Per Serving
Calories: 230 | fat: 15g | protein: 11g | carbs: 13g | fiber: 1g | sodium: 510mg

2. Savory Feta, Spinach, and Red Pepper Muffins
Prep time: 10 minutes | Cook time: 22 minutes | Serves 12

250g all-purpose flour
94g whole-wheat flour
31g granulated sugar
10g baking powder
2g paprika
5g salt
125ml extra virgin olive oil
2 eggs
188ml skimmed milk
188g crumbled feta
83g jarred red peppers, drained, patted dry, and chopped

1. Preheat the oven to 375°F (190°C) and line a large muffin pan with 12 muffin liners.
2. In a large bowl, combine the all-purpose flour, whole-wheat flour, sugar, baking powder, paprika, and salt. Mix well.
3. In a medium bowl, whisk the olive oil, eggs, and milk.
4. Add the wet ingredients to the dry ingredients, and use a wooden spoon to stir until the ingredients are just blended and form a thick dough.
5. Add the feta, spinach, and peppers, and mix gently until all the ingredients are incorporated. Evenly divide the mixture among the muffin liners.
6. Transfer to the oven, and bake for 25 minutes or until a toothpick inserted into the middle of a muffin comes out clean.
7. Set the muffins aside to cool for 10 minutes, and remove them from the pan. Store in an airtight container in the refrigerator for up to 3 days. (Remove from

the refrigerator 10 minutes before consuming.)

Per Serving

Calories: 243 | fat: 12g | protein:6g | carbs: 27g | fiber: 2g | sodium: 306mg

3. Spinach and Mushroom Mini Quiche

Prep time: 10 minutes | Cook time: 15 minutes | Serves 4

5ml olive oil, plus more for spraying

125g coarsely chopped mushrooms

125g fresh baby spinach, shredded

4 eggs, beaten

125g shredded Cheddar cheese

125g shredded Mozzarella cheese

2g salt

0.5g black pepper

1. Spray 4 silicone baking cups with olive oil and set aside.
2. In a medium sauté pan over medium heat, warm 5ml olive oil. Add the mushrooms and sauté until soft, 3 to 4 minutes.
3. Add the spinach and cook until wilted, 1 to 2 minutes. Set aside.
4. In a medium bowl, whisk together the eggs, Cheddar cheese, Mozzarella cheese, salt, and pepper.
5. Gently fold the mushrooms and spinach into the egg mixture.
6. Pour ¼ of the mixture into each silicone baking cup.
7. Place the baking cups into the air fryer basket and air fry at 350°F (177°C) for 5 minutes. Stir the mixture in each ramekin slightly and air fry until the egg has set, an additional 3 to 5 minutes.

Per Serving

Calories: 156 | fat: 10g | protein: 14g | carbs: 2g | fiber: 1g | sodium: 411mg

4. Broccoli-Mushroom Frittata

Prep time: 10 minutes | Cook time: 20 minutes | Serves 2

15ml olive oil

188g broccoli florets, finely chopped

63g sliced brown mushrooms

31g finely chopped onion

3g salt

0.5g freshly ground black pepper

6 eggs

63g Parmesan cheese

1. In a nonstick cake pan, combine the olive oil, broccoli, mushrooms, onion, salt, and pepper. Stir until the vegetables are thoroughly coated with oil. Place the cake pan in the air fryer basket and set the air fryer to 400°F (204°C). Air fry for 5 minutes until the vegetables soften.
2. Meanwhile, in a medium bowl, whisk the eggs and Parmesan until thoroughly combined. Pour the egg mixture into the pan and shake gently to distribute the vegetables. Air fry for another 15 minutes until the eggs are set. 3. Remove from the air fryer and let sit for 5 minutes to cool slightly. Use a silicone spatula to gently lift the frittata onto a plate before serving.

Per Serving

Calories: 329 | fat: 23g | protein: 24g | carbs: 6g | fiber: 0g | sodium: 793mg

5. Tomato, Basil & Parmesan Scrambled Eggs

Prep time: 5 minutes | Cook time: 10 minutes | Serves 1

3 eggs

15ml olive oil

50g cherry tomatoes, halved

handful of fresh basil leaves, chopped

25g Parmesan cheese, grated

salt and freshly ground black pepper

1. Whisk the eggs in a bowl with a little salt and pepper.
2. Heat the olive oil in a frying pan over a medium heat and add the cherry tomatoes. Cook for 1-2 minutes until beginning to soften.
3. Add the eggs to the pan and cook, stirring frequently, until scrambled and cooked to your liking.
4. Stir in the basil and Parmesan and serve immediately.

Per Serving

Calories: 463| fat: 37.6g | protein: 26.3g |carbs: 8g | fiber: 1.7g |sodium:589mg

6. Mediterranean Breakfast Salad

Prep time: 10 minutes | Cook time: N/A | Serves 4

225g uncooked breakfast sausage

1/4 onion, diced

60g mushrooms, diced

45g sun-dried tomatoes, diced

4 eggs, beaten

120g feta cheese, crumbled

180g grape tomatoes, halved

6 kalamata olives, pitted and halved

3.8g chopped fresh parsley

Salt and black pepper to taste

1. In a large skillet over medium heat, cook sausage, onion, mushrooms, and sun-dried tomatoes until sausage is cooked through and vegetables are softened, about 5 minutes.
2. Add eggs to the pan and scramble until cooked through. Remove from heat and stir in feta cheese.
3. To serve, divide egg mixture evenly among 4 plates. Top with grape tomatoes, olives, parsley, salt, and black pepper.

Per Serving

Calories: 487 | fat: 37g | protein: 28g | carbs: 15g | fiber: 3g | sodium: 1339mg

7. Red Pepper and Feta Frittata

Prep time: 10 minutes | Cook time: 20 minutes | Serves 4

Olive oil cooking spray

8 large eggs

1 medium red bell pepper, diced

3g salt

1g black pepper

1 garlic clove, minced

126g feta, divided

1. Preheat the air fryer to 360°F(182°C). Lightly coat the inside of a 6-inch round cake pan with olive oil cooking spray.

2. In a large bowl, beat the eggs for 1 to 2 minutes, or until well combined.

3. Add the bell pepper, salt, black pepper, and garlic to the eggs, and mix together until the bell pepper is distributed throughout.

4. Fold in 63g the feta cheese.

5. Pour the egg mixture into the prepared cake pan, and sprinkle the remaining 63g feta over the top.

6. Place into the air fryer and bake for 18 to 20 minutes, or until the eggs are set in the center.

7. Remove from the air fryer and allow to cool for 5 minutes before serving.

Per Serving

Calories: 204 | fat: 14g | protein: 16g | carbs: 4g | fiber: 1g | sodium: 606mg

8. Spinach and Feta Frittata

Prep time: 10 minutes | Cook time: 26 minutes | Serves 4

15ml olive oil

½ medium onion, peeled and chopped

½ medium red bell pepper, seeded and chopped

250g chopped fresh baby spinach

250ml water

250g crumbled feta cheese

6 large eggs, beaten

63g low-fat plain Greek yogurt

3g salt

1g ground black pepper

1. Press the Sauté button on the Instant Pot® and heat oil. Add onion and bell pepper, and cook until tender, about 8 minutes. Add spinach and cook until wilted, about 3 minutes. Press the Cancel button and transfer vegetables to a medium bowl to cool. Wipe out inner pot.

2. Place the rack in the Instant Pot® and add water. Spray a 1.5-liter baking dish with nonstick cooking spray. Drain excess liquid from spinach mixture, then add to dish with cheese.

3. In a separate medium bowl, mix eggs, yogurt, salt, and black pepper until well combined. Pour over vegetable and cheese mixture. Cover dish tightly with foil, then gently lower into machine.

4. Close lid, set steam release to Sealing, press the Manual button, and set time to 15 minutes. When the timer beeps, let pressure release naturally for 10 minutes, then quick-release any remaining pressure until the float valve drops. Press the Cancel button and open lid. Let stand for 10–15 minutes before carefully removing dish from pot.

5.Run a thin knife around the edge of the frittata and turn it out onto a serving platter. Serve warm.

Per Serving

Calories: 259 | fat: 19g | protein: 16g | carbs: 6g | fiber: 1g | sodium: 766mg

9. Greek Yogurt Parfait

Prep time: 5 minutes | Cook time: 0 minutes | Serves 1

125g plain whole-milk Greek yogurt

36g double cream

31g frozen berries, thawed with juices

0.5g vanilla or almond extract (optional)

1g ground cinnamon (optional)

7g ground flax seed

30g chopped nuts (walnuts or pecans)

1. In a small bowl or glass, combine the yogurt, heavy whipping cream, thawed berries in their juice, vanilla or almond extract (if using), cinnamon (if using), and flax seed and stir well until smooth. Top with chopped nuts and enjoy.

Per Serving

Calories: 333 | fat: 27g | protein: 10g | carbs: 15g | fiber: 4g | sodium: 71mg

10. Power Peach Smoothie Bowl

Prep time: 15 minutes | Cook time: 0 minutes | Serves 2

250g packed partially thawed frozen peaches

125g plain or vanilla Greek yogurt

½ ripe avocado

14g flax meal

1g vanilla extract

5g orange extract

15g honey (optional)

1. Combine all of the ingredients in a blender and blend until smooth.
2. Pour the mixture into two bowls, and, if desired, sprinkle with additional toppings.

Per Serving

Calories: 213 | fat: 13g | protein: 6g | carbs: 23g | fiber: 7g | sodium: 41mg

11. Amaranth Breakfast Bowl with Chocolate and Almonds

Prep time: 10 minutes | Cook time: 6 minutes | Serves 6

250g amaranth, rinsed and drained

500ml almond milk

500ml water

63ml maple syrup

21g cocoa powder

1g vanilla extract

2g salt

63g toasted sliced almonds

41g milk chocolate chips

1. Place amaranth, almond milk, water, maple syrup, cocoa powder, vanilla, and salt in the Instant Pot®. Stir to combine. Close lid, set steam release to Sealing, press the Rice button, and set time to 6 minutes. When the timer beeps, quick-release the pressure until the float valve drops, press the Cancel button, open lid, and stir well.
2. Serve hot, topped with almonds and chocolate chips.

Per Serving

Calories: 263 | fat: 12g | protein: 5g | carbs: 35g | fiber: 5g | sodium: 212mg

12. Portobello Eggs Benedict

Prep time: 10 minutes | Cook time: 10 to 14 minutes | Serves 2

15ml olive oil

2 cloves garlic, minced

0.3g dried thyme

2 portobello mushrooms, stems removed and gills scraped out

2 plum tomatoes, halved lengthwise

Pinch salt and freshly ground black pepper, to taste

2 large eggs

36g grated Pecorino Romano cheese

4g chopped fresh parsley, for garnish

5ml truffle oil (optional)

1. Preheat the air fryer to 400°F (204°C).
2. In a small bowl, combine the olive oil, garlic, and thyme. Brush the mixture over the mushrooms and tomatoes until thoroughly coated. Season to taste with salt and freshly ground black pepper.
3. Arrange the vegetables, cut side up, in the air fryer basket. Crack an egg into the center of each mushroom and sprinkle with cheese. Air fry for 10 to 14 minutes until the vegetables are tender and the whites are firm. When cool enough to handle, coarsely chop the tomatoes and place on top of the eggs. Scatter parsley on top and drizzle with truffle oil, if desired, just before serving.

Per Serving

Calories: 189 | fat: 13g | protein: 11g | carbs: 7g | fiber: 2g | sodium: 87mg

Chapter 3 Beef, Pork, and Lamb

13. Roast Pork Tenderloin with Cherry-Balsamic Sauce

Prep time : 20 minutes | Cook Time: 20 minutes | Serves 2

125g frozen cherries, thawed

83ml balsamic vinegar

1 fresh rosemary sprig

1 (227g) pork tenderloin

1.5g salt

0.5g freshly ground black pepper

15ml olive oil

1. Combine the cherries and vinegar in a blender and purée until smooth.
2. Pour into a saucepan, add the rosemary sprig, and bring the mixture to a boil. Reduce the heat to medium-low and simmer for 15 minutes, or until it's reduced by half.
3. While the sauce is simmering, preheat the oven to 425°F (220°C) and set

the rack in the middle position.

4. Season the pork on all sides with the salt and pepper.

5. Heat the oil in a sauté pan over medium-high heat. Add the pork and sear for 3 minutes, turning often, until it's golden on all sides.

6. Transfer the pork to an oven-safe baking dish and roast for 15 minutes, or until the internal temperature is 145°F(63°C).

7. Let the pork rest for 5 minutes before serving. Serve sliced and topped with the cherry-balsamic sauce.

Per Serving

Calories: 328 | fat: 11g | protein: 21g | carbs: 30g | fiber: 1g | sodium: 386mg

14. Bulgur and Beef–Stuffed Peppers

Prep time: 15 minutes | Cook time: 26 minutes | Serves 4

63g bulgur wheat

250ml vegetable stock

30ml olive oil

1 medium white onion, peeled and diced

1 clove garlic, peeled and minced

1 medium plum tomato, seeded and chopped

1g minced fresh rosemary

1g fresh thyme leaves

3g salt

1g ground black pepper

227g 90% lean ground beef

4 large red bell peppers, tops removed and seeded

125g ready-made tomato sauce

250ml water

125g grated Parmesan cheese

1. Add bulgur and broth to the Instant Pot® and stir well. Close lid, set steam release to Sealing, press the Rice button, adjust pressure to Low, and set time to 12 minutes. When the timer beeps, quick-release the pressure until the float valve drops. Open lid and fluff bulgur with a fork, then transfer to a medium bowl and set aside to cool.

2. Press the Sauté button and heat oil. Add onion and cook until tender, about 5 minutes. Add garlic, tomato, rosemary, thyme, salt, and pepper. Cook until garlic and herbs are fragrant, about 1 minute.

3. Add ground beef and cook, crumbling well, until no longer pink, about 5 minutes. Press the Cancel button.

4. Add beef mixture to bulgur and mix well. Divide mixture between bell peppers, making sure not to compact the mixture too much. Top each pepper with marinara sauce.

5. Clean out pot, add water, and place rack in pot. Carefully stand peppers on rack. Close lid, set steam release to Sealing, press the Manual button, and set time to 3 minutes. When the timer beeps, quick-release the pressure until the float valve drops. Open lid and carefully transfer peppers with tongs to plates. Top with cheese and serve immediately

Per Serving

Calories: 363 | fat: 17g | protein: 21g | carbs: 31g | fiber: 7g | sodium: 594mg

15. Beef, Mushroom, and Green Bean Soup

Prep time: 10 minutes | Cook time: 45 minutes | Serves 4

30ml olive oil

454g chuck or round beef roast, cut into 2-inch pieces

1 large onion, diced

3g sea salt

0.5g freshly ground black pepper

125ml white wine

2000ml chicken stock

454 g green beans

227 g cremini (baby bella) mushrooms, chopped

54g tomato paste

0.5g dried oregano

1. In a large stockpot, heat the olive oil over medium-high heat. Add the beef and brown, 5 to 7 minutes. Add the onion, salt, and pepper and cook for 5 minutes. Add the wine and cook for 4 minutes. Add the broth, green beans, mushrooms, tomato paste, and oregano and stir to combine.

2. Bring to a boil, reduce the heat to low, cover, and simmer for 35 to 45

minutes, until the meat is cooked through. Serve.

Per Serving

Calories: 307 | fat: 14g | protein: 28g | carbs: 17g | fiber: 5g | sodium: 265mg

16. Fajita Meatball Lettuce Wraps

Prep time: 10 minutes | Cook time: 10 minutes | Serves 4

454g minced beef (85% lean)

125g salsa, plus more for serving if desired

31g chopped onions

31g diced green or red bell peppers

1 large egg, beaten

6g fine sea salt

1g chili powder

1g ground cumin

1 clove garlic, minced

For Serving (Optional):

8 leaves butterhead lettuce

Pico de gallo or salsa

Lime slices

1. Spray the air fryer basket with avocado oil. Preheat the air fryer to 350°F (177°C).
2. In a large bowl, mix together all the ingredients until well combined.
3. Shape the meat mixture into eight 1-inch balls. Place the meatballs in the air fryer basket, leaving a little space between them. Air fry for 10 minutes, or until cooked through and no longer pink inside and the internal temperature reaches 145°F (63°C).
4. Serve each meatball on a lettuce leaf, topped with pico de gallo or salsa, if desired. Serve with lime slices if desired.
5. Store leftovers in an airtight container in the fridge for 3 days or in the freezer for up to a month. Reheat in a preheated 350°F (177°C) air fryer for 4 minutes, or until heated through.

Per Serving

Calories: 289 | fat: 20g | protein: 24g | carbs: 4g | fiber: 1g | sodium: 815mg

17. Spiced Lamb Stew with Fennel and Dates

Prep time: 10 minutes | Cook time: 3 hours | Serves 4

30ml olive oil, divided

1 fennel bulb, trimmed, cored, and thinly sliced

1 red onion, thinly sliced

2 cloves garlic, thinly sliced

680g lamb shoulder, cut into 1½-inch cubes and dried with paper towels

5g ground ginger

5g ground cumin

2g ground coriander

1g cayenne pepper

6g salt

125g pitted chopped dates

500ml water, divided

5g chopped cilantro, for garnish

1. Heat 15ml olive oil in a Dutch oven. Add the fennel, onion, and garlic and cook, stirring frequently, until softened and beginning to brown, about 7 minutes. Transfer the vegetables to a plate.
2. Add the remaining 15ml olive oil to the pot and cook the lamb, turning every couple of minutes, until browned on all sides.
3. In a small bowl, combine the ginger, cumin, coriander, cayenne, and salt and mix well. Sprinkle the spice mixture over the meat in the pot and cook, stirring, for 1 minute.
4. Return the vegetables to the pot and add the dates and 250ml water. Reduce the heat to medium-low, cover, and cook, stirring occasionally and adding the remaining 250ml water as needed, for 2½ hours, until the lamb is very tender and the sauce has thickened. Serve immediately, garnished with cilantro.

Per Serving

Calories: 539 | fat: 20g | protein: 50g | carbs: 52g | fiber: 6g | sodium: 749mg

18. Lemon, Potato And Olive Baked Lamb With Pangrattato

Prep time: 10 minutes | Cook time: 1 hours | Serves 4

15ml olive oil, plus extra for drizzling

0.9g onion, diced

3 garlic cloves, peeled and crushed

0.6g red bell pepper, diced

0.3g yellow bell pepper, diced

450g lamb stewing meat

1 lemon, thinly sliced

250g potatoes, thinly sliced

100g black olives

Salt and freshly ground black pepper

50g pangrattato (breadcrumbs)

Lemon wedges, to serve

1. Preheat the oven to 180°C/350°F/Gas 4.
2. Heat the oil in a large frying pan over medium heat. Add the onion, garlic and bell peppers and fry for 2-3 minutes.
3. Add the lamb and fry for 5-6 minutes, or until browned all over.
4. In a large baking dish, layer the lemon slices, potatoes, olives and lamb. Season with salt and pepper.
5. Drizzle with olive oil and bake in the oven for 1 hour.
6. Remove from the oven and sprinkle with pangrattato. Drizzle with additional olive oil, if desired. Serve immediately with lemon wedges, if desired.

Per Serving

Calories: 446|fat: 24.4g |protein: 32.5g |carbs: 22.6g |fiber: 3.7g|sodium:85mg

19. Zesty Grilled Flank Steak

Prep time: 10 minutes | Cook time: 18 minutes | Serves 6

63ml olive oil

45ml red wine vinegar

1g dried rosemary

1g dried marjoram

1g dried oregano

2g paprika

2 cloves garlic, minced

2g freshly ground pepper

907g flank steak

1. Combine the olive oil, vinegar, herbs, and seasonings in a small bowl. Place the flank steak in a shallow dish, and rub the marinade into the meat. Cover and refrigerate for up to 24 hours.
2. Heat a charcoal or gas grill to medium heat (375°F / 190°C).
3. Grill the steak for 18–21 minutes, turning once halfway through the cooking time.
4. An internal meat thermometer should read 140°F (60°C) when the meat is done.
5. Transfer the meat to a cutting board, and cover with aluminum foil. Let steak rest for at least 10 minutes.
6. Slice against the grain very thinly and serve.

Per Serving

Calories: 292 | fat: 17g | protein: 33g | carbs: 1g | fiber: 0g | sodium: 81mg

20. Pork Tenderloin with Chermoula Sauce

Prep Time: 15 minutes | Cook Time: 20 minutes | Serves 2

31g fresh parsley

10g fresh coriander

6 small garlic cloves

45ml olive oil, divided

45ml freshly squeezed lemon juice

5g smoked paprika

5g cumin

3g salt, divided

Pinch freshly ground black pepper

1 (227g) pork tenderloin

1. Preheat the oven to 425°F (220°C) and set the rack to the middle position. 2. In the bowl of a food processor, combine the parsley, cilantro, garlic, 30ml olive oil, the lemon juice, paprika, cumin, and 1g salt. Pulse 15 to 20 times, or until the mixture is fairly smooth. Scrape the sides down as needed to incorporate all of the ingredients. Transfer the sauce to a small bowl and set aside.

2. Season the pork tenderloin on all sides with the remaining 1g salt and a generous pinch of pepper.

3. Heat the remaining 15ml olive oil in a sauté pan. Add the pork and sear for 3 minutes, turning often, until it's golden on all sides.

5. Transfer the pork to an oven-safe baking dish and roast for 15 minutes, or until the internal temperature registers 145°F (63°C).

Per Serving

Calories: 168 | fat: 13g | protein: 11g | carbs: 3g | fiber: 1g | sodium: 333mg

21. Beef Kofta

Prep time: 10 minutes | Cook time: 20 minutes | Serves 4

Olive oil cooking spray

½ onion, roughly chopped

1-inch piece ginger, peeled

2 garlic cloves, peeled

21g fresh parsley

7g fresh mint

454g ground beef

7g ground cumin

3g ground coriander

3g ground cinnamon

4g coarse sea salt

1g ground sumac

0.5g ground cloves

0.5g freshly ground black pepper

1. Preheat the oven to 400°F (205°C). Grease a 3000ml muffin tin with olive oil cooking spray.

2. In a food processor, add the onion, ginger, garlic, parsley, and mint; process until minced.

3. Place the onion mixture in a large bowl. Add the beef, cumin, coriander, cinnamon, salt, sumac, cloves, and black pepper and mix together thoroughly with your hands.

4. Divide the beef mixture into 12 balls and place each one in a cup of the prepared muffin tin. Bake for 20 minutes.

Per Serving

Calories: 225 | fat: 12g | protein: g24 | carbs: 5g | fiber: 2g | sodium: 290mg

22. Spanish Meatballs

Prep time: 10 minutes | Cook time: 5 hours 10 minutes | Serves 8

907g minced pork

1 medium yellow onion, finely chopped

4g ground cumin

3g hot smoked paprika

75g plain dried bread crumbs

2 large eggs, lightly beaten

12g chopped fresh parsley

Pinch coarse sea salt

Pinch black pepper

45ml extra-virgin olive oil

1 (794g) can diced tomatoes, with the juice

Rustic bread, for serving (optional)

1. In a large bowl, combine the pork, 31g the onion, cumin, 3g the paprika, bread crumbs, eggs, and parsley. Season with the salt and pepper. Mix thoroughly to combine.
2. Roll the meat mixture into 25 meatballs (each about 1½ inches), and put on a plate.
3. In a large nonstick skillet, heat 23ml the olive oil over medium-high heat. In two batches, brown the meatballs on all sides, 8 minutes per batch. Transfer the browned meatballs to the slow cooker.
4. Add the remaining onion to the skillet, and cook until fragrant, stirring often, about 2 minutes. Transfer the onion to the slow cooker, sprinkle in the remaining 5g paprika, and add the tomatoes. Season with salt and pepper.
5. Cover and cook on low until the meatballs are tender, 5 hours. Serve with slices of rustic bread, if desired.

Per Serving

Calories: 241 | fat: 11g | protein: 27g | carbs: 9g | fiber: 3g | sodium: 137mg

23. Spicy Lamb Sirloin Chops

Prep time: 30 minutes | Cook time: 15 minutes | Serves 4

½ yellow onion, coarsely chopped

4 coin-size slices peeled fresh ginger

5 garlic cloves

2g garam masala

2g ground fennel

3g ground cinnamon

3g ground turmeric

1g to 2g cayenne pepper

1g ground cardamom

6g coarse sea salt

454g lamb sirloin chops

1. In a blender, combine the onion, ginger, garlic, garam masala, fennel, cinnamon, turmeric, cayenne, cardamom, and salt. Pulse until the onion is finely minced and the mixture forms a thick paste, 3 to 4 minutes.
2. Place the lamb chops in a large bowl. Slash the meat and fat with a sharp knife several times to allow the marinade to penetrate better. Add the spice paste to the bowl and toss the lamb to coat. Marinate at room temperature for 30 minutes or cover and refrigerate for up to 24 hours.
3. Place the lamb chops in a single layer in the air fryer basket. Set the air fryer to 325°F (163°C) for 15 minutes, turning the chops halfway through the cooking time. Use a meat thermometer to ensure the lamb has reached an internal temperature of 145°F (63°C) (medium-rare).

Per Serving

Calories: 179 | fat: 7g | protein: 24g | carbs: 4g | fiber: 1g | sodium: 657mg

24. Lamb Stew

Prep time: 20 minutes | Cook time: 2 hours 20 minutes | Serves 6

3 carrots, peeled and sliced

2 onions, minced

500ml white wine

31g flat-leaf parsley, chopped

2 garlic cloves, minced

3 bay leaves

1g dried rosemary leaves

0.3g nutmeg

0.5g ground cloves

907g boneless lamb, cut into 1-inch pieces

62ml olive oil

1 jar artichoke hearts

Pinch sea salt and freshly ground pepper, to taste

1. Combine the carrots, onion, white wine, parsley, garlic, bay leaves, and seasonings in a plastic bag or shallow dish.
2. Add the lamb and marinate overnight.
3. Drain the lamb, reserving the marinade, and pat dry.
4. Heat the olive oil in a large stew pot. Brown the lamb meat, turning frequently.
5. Pour the marinade into the stew pot, cover, and simmer on low for 2 hours.
6. Add the artichoke hearts and simmer an additional 20 minutes. Season with sea salt and freshly ground pepper.

Per Serving

Calories: 399 | fat: 18g | protein: 33g | carbs: 13g | fiber: 3g | sodium: 167mg

25. Seasoned Beef Kebabs

Prep time: 15 minutes | Cook time: 10 minutes | Serves 6

907g beef fillet

9g salt

2g freshly ground black pepper

1g ground allspice

1g ground nutmeg

83ml extra-virgin olive oil

1 large onion, cut into 8 quarters

1 large red bell pepper, cut into 1-inch cubes

1. Preheat a grill, grill pan, or lightly oiled skillet to high heat.
2. Cut the beef into 1-inch cubes and put them in a large bowl.
3. In a small bowl, mix together the salt, black pepper, allspice, and nutmeg. 4. Pour the olive oil over the beef and toss to coat the beef. Then evenly sprinkle

the seasoning over the beef and toss to coat all pieces.

5.Skewer the beef, alternating every 1 or 2 pieces with a piece of onion or bell pepper.

6. To cook, place the skewers on the grill or skillet, and turn every 2 to 3 minutes until all sides have cooked to desired doneness, 6 minutes for medium-rare, 8 minutes for well done. Serve warm.

Per Serving

Calories: 326 | fat: 21g | protein: 32g | carbs: 4g | fiber: 1g | sodium: 714mg

Chapter 4 Poultry

26. Crispy Dill Chicken Strips

Prep time: 30 minutes | Cook time: 10 minutes | Serves 4

2 whole boneless, skinless chicken breasts (about 454g each), halved lengthwise

250g Italian dressing

375g finely crushed potato chips

3g dried dill weed

5g garlic powder

1 large egg, beaten

15ml to 30ml oil

1. In a large resealable bag, combine the chicken and Italian dressing. Seal the bag and refrigerate to marinate at least 1 hour.
2. In a shallow dish, stir together the potato chips, dill, and garlic powder. Place the beaten egg in a second shallow dish.
3. Remove the chicken from the marinade. Roll the chicken pieces in the egg and the potato chip mixture, coating thoroughly.
4. Preheat the air fryer to 325°F (163°C). Line the air fryer basket with parchment paper.
5. Place the coated chicken on the parchment and spritz with oil.
6. Cook for 5 minutes. Flip the chicken, spritz it with oil, and cook for 5 minutes more until the outsides are crispy and the insides are no longer pink.

Per Serving

Calories: 349 | fat: 16g | protein: 30g | carbs: 20g | fiber: 2g | sodium: 92mg

27. Citrus and Spice Chicken

Prep time: 15 minutes | Cook time: 17 minutes | Serves 8

30ml olive oil

1.4kg boneless, skinless chicken thighs

2g smoked paprika

3g salt

0.4g ground cinnamon

0.4g ground ginger

0.3g ground nutmeg

63g golden raisins

63g flaked almonds

250ml orange juice

31ml lemon juice

31ml lime juice

454g carrots, peeled and chopped

30ml water

8g arrowroot powder

1. Press the Sauté button on the Instant Pot® and heat oil. Fry chicken thighs for 2 minutes on each side until browned.
2. Add paprika, salt, cinnamon, ginger, nutmeg, raisins, almonds, orange juice, lemon juice, lime juice, and carrots. Press the Cancel button.
3. Close lid, set steam release to Sealing, press the Manual button, and set time to 10 minutes. When the timer beeps, let pressure release naturally for 5 minutes. Quick-release any remaining pressure until the float valve drops and then open lid. Check chicken using a meat thermometer to make sure the internal temperature is at least 165°F (74°C).
4. Use a slotted spoon to remove chicken, carrots, and raisins, and transfer to a serving platter. Press the Cancel button.
5. In a small bowl, whisk together water and arrowroot to create a slurry. Add to liquid in the Instant Pot® and stir to combine. Press the Sauté button, press the Adjust button to change the temperature to Less, and simmer uncovered for 3 minutes until sauce is thickened. Pour sauce over chicken and serve.

Per Serving

Calories: 332 | fat: 14g | protein: 36g | carbs: 14g | fiber: 3g | sodium: 337mg

28. Lemon-Basil Turkey Breasts

Prep time: 30 minutes | Cook time: 58 minutes | Serves 4

30ml olive oil

907g turkey breasts, bone-in, skin-on

Pinch coarse sea salt and ground black pepper, to taste

1g fresh basil leaves, chopped

12g lemon zest, grated

1. Rub olive oil on all sides of the turkey breasts; sprinkle with salt, pepper, basil, and lemon zest.
2. Place the turkey breasts skin side up on the parchment-lined air fryer basket.
3. Cook in the preheated air fryer at 330°F (166°C) for 30 minutes. Now, turn them over and cook an additional 28 minutes.
4. Serve with lemon wedges, if desired. Bon appétit!

Per Serving

Calories: 417 | fat: 23g | protein: 50g | carbs: 0g | fiber: 0g | sodium: 134mg

29. Chicken and Broccoli Casserole

Prep time: 5 minutes | Cook time: 20 to 25 minutes | Serves 4

227g broccoli, chopped into florets

250g shredded cooked chicken

113g cream cheese

83g double cream

8g Dijon mustard

3g garlic powder

Pinch salt and freshly ground black pepper, to taste

6g chopped fresh basil

250g shredded Cheddar cheese

1. Preheat the air fryer to 390°F (199°C). Lightly coat a casserole dish that will fit in air fryer, with olive oil and set aside.
2. Place the broccoli in a large glass bowl with 15ml water and cover with a microwavable plate. Microwave on high for 2 to 3 minutes until the broccoli is bright green but not mushy. Drain if necessary and add to another large bowl along with the shredded chicken.

3. In the same glass bowl used to microwave the broccoli, combine the cream cheese and cream. Microwave for 30 seconds to 1 minute on high and stir until smooth. Add the mustard and garlic powder and season to taste with salt and freshly ground black pepper. Whisk until the sauce is smooth.

4. Pour the warm sauce over the broccoli and chicken mixture and then add the basil. Using a silicone spatula, gently fold the mixture until thoroughly combined.

5. Transfer the chicken mixture to the prepared casserole dish and top with the cheese. Air fry for 20 to 25 minutes until warmed through and the cheese has browned.

Per Serving

Calories: 503 | fat: 39g | protein: 32g | carbs: 7g | fiber: 2g | sodium: 391mg

30. Spinach and Feta Stuffed Chicken Breasts

Prep time: 10 minutes | Cook time: 27 minutes | Serves 4

1 (283g) package frozen spinach, thawed and drained well

250g feta cheese, crumbled

1g freshly ground black pepper

4 boneless chicken breasts

Pinch salt and freshly ground black pepper, to taste

15ml olive oil

1. Prepare the filling. Squeeze out as much liquid as possible from the thawed spinach. Rough chop the spinach and transfer it to a mixing bowl with the feta cheese and the freshly ground black pepper.

2. Prepare the chicken breast. Place the chicken breast on a cutting board and press down on the chicken breast with one hand to keep it stabilized. Make an incision about 1-inch long in the fattest side of the breast. Move the knife up and down inside the chicken breast, without poking through either the top or the bottom, or the other side of the breast. The inside pocket should be about 3-inches long, but the opening should only be about 1-inch wide. If this is too difficult, you can make the incision longer, but you will have to be more careful when cooking the chicken breast since this will expose more of the stuffing.

3. Once you have prepared the chicken breasts, use your fingers to stuff the filling into each pocket, spreading the mixture down as far as you can.

4. Preheat the air fryer to 380°F (193°C).

5. Lightly brush or spray the air fryer basket and the chicken breasts with olive oil. Transfer two of the stuffed chicken breasts to the air fryer. Air fry for 12 minutes, turning the chicken breasts over halfway through the cooking time. Remove the chicken to a resting plate and air fry the second two breasts for 12 minutes. Return the first batch of chicken to the air fryer with the second batch and air fry for 3 more minutes. When the chicken is cooked, an instant read thermometer should register 165°F (74°C) in the thickest part of the chicken, as well as in the stuffing.

6. Remove the chicken breasts and let them rest on a cutting board for 2 to 3 minutes. Slice the chicken on the bias and serve with the slices fanned out.

Per Serving

Calories: 476 | fat: 19g | protein: 69g | carbs: 5g | fiber: 2g | sodium: 519mg

31. Turkey Meatloaf

Prep time: 10 minutes | Cook time: 50 minutes | Serves 4

227g sliced mushrooms

1 small onion, coarsely chopped

2 cloves garlic

680g 85% lean minced turkey

2 eggs, lightly beaten

18g tomato paste

25g ground almonds

30ml almond milk

3g dried oregano

6g salt

1g freshly ground black pepper

1 plum tomato, thinly sliced

1. Preheat the air fryer to 350°F (177°C). Lightly coat a round pan with olive oil and set aside.

2. In a food processor fitted with a metal blade, combine the mushrooms, onion, and garlic. Pulse until finely chopped. Transfer the vegetables to a large mixing bowl.

3. Add the turkey, eggs, tomato paste, almond meal, milk, oregano, salt, and

black pepper. Mix gently until thoroughly combined. Transfer the mixture to the prepared pan and shape into a loaf. Arrange the tomato slices on top.

4. Air fry for 50 minutes or until the meatloaf is nicely browned and a thermometer inserted into the thickest part registers 165°F (74°C). Remove from the air fryer and let rest for about 10 minutes before slicing.

Per Serving

Calories: 353 | fat: 20g | protein: 38g | carbs: 7g | fiber: 2g | sodium: 625mg

32. Chicken Pesto Pizzas

Prep time: 10 minutes | Cook time: 12 minutes | Serves 4

454g minced chicken

1g salt

0.5g ground black pepper

63g basil pesto

250g shredded Mozzarella cheese

4 grape tomatoes, sliced

1. Cut four squares of parchment paper to fit into your air fryer basket.

2. Place ground chicken in a large bowl and mix with salt and pepper. Divide mixture into four equal sections.

3. Wet your hands with water to prevent sticking, then press each section into a 6-inch circle onto a piece of ungreased parchment. Place each chicken crust into air fryer basket, working in batches if needed.

4. Adjust the temperature to 350°F (177°C) and air fry for 10 minutes, turning crusts halfway through cooking.

5. Spread 18g pesto across the top of each crust, then sprinkle with 63g Mozzarella and top with 1 sliced tomato. Continue cooking at 350°F (177°C) for 2 minutes. Cheese will be melted and brown when done. Serve warm.

Per Serving

Calories: 302 | fat: 18g | protein: 32g | carbs: 2g | fiber: 0g | sodium: 398mg

33. Chicken in Lemon and Herb Sauce

Prep time: 10 minutes | Cook time: 24 minutes | Serves 4

30ml olive oil

454g boneless, skinless chicken breast, cut in 1" pieces

125ml low-sodium chicken stock

30ml lemon juice

2 cloves garlic, peeled and minced

10g Dijon mustard

5g Italian seasoning

3g salt

6g grated lemon zest

4g chopped fresh parsley

1. Press the Sauté button on the Instant Pot® and heat oil. Add chicken and cook for about 4 minutes or until lightly browned on all sides. Stir in broth, lemon juice, garlic, mustard, Italian seasoning, and salt. Press the Cancel button.
2. Close lid, set steam release to Sealing, press the Poultry button, and cook for the default time of 15 minutes. When the timer beeps, let pressure release naturally for 10 minutes. Quick-release any remaining pressure until the float valve drops and then open lid. Check chicken using a meat thermometer to ensure the internal temperature is at least 165°F(74°C). Transfer chicken to a serving platter. Press the Cancel button.
3. Press the Sauté button, press the Adjust button to change the temperature to Less, and simmer uncovered for 5 minutes to thicken sauce, then pour sauce over chicken.
4. Garnish with lemon zest and chopped parsley. Serve warm.

Per Serving

Calories: 235 | fat: 11g | protein: 35g | carbs: 0g | fiber: 0g | sodium: 371mg

34. Tahini Chicken Rice Bowls

Prep time: 10 minutes |Cook time: 15 minutes| Serves: 4

125g uncooked instant brown rice

60g tahini or peanut butter (tahini for nut-free)

63g 2% plain Greek yogurt

30g chopped spring onions, green and white parts (2 spring onions)

15ml freshly squeezed lemon juice (from ½ medium lemon)

15ml water

5g ground cumin

4g ground cinnamon

1g coarse sea salt

about 454g chopped cooked chicken breast

63g chopped dried apricots

250g peeled and chopped seedless cucumber (1 large cucumber)

12g sesame seeds

Fresh mint leaves, for serving (optional)

1. Cook the brown rice according to the package instructions.
2. While the rice is cooking, in a medium bowl, mix together the tahini, yogurt, scallions, lemon juice, water, cumin, cinnamon, and salt. Transfer half the tahini mixture to another medium bowl. Mix the chicken into the first bowl.
3. When the rice is done, mix it into the second bowl of tahini (the one without the chicken).
4. To assemble, divide the chicken among four bowls. Spoon the rice mixture next to the chicken in each bowl. Next to the chicken, place the dried apricots, and in the remaining empty section, add the cucumbers. Sprinkle with sesame seeds, and top with mint, if desired, and serve.

Per Serving

Calories: 448 | fat: 13g | protein: 30g | carbs: 53g | fiber: 5g | sodium: 243mg

35. Classic Whole Chicken

Prep time: 5 minutes | Cook time: 50 minutes | Serves 4

Oil, for spraying

1 (1.8kg) whole chicken, giblets removed

15ml olive oil

3g paprika

2g granulated garlic

3g salt

1g freshly ground black pepper

0.5g finely chopped fresh parsley, for garnish

1. Line the air fryer basket with parchment and spray lightly with oil.
2. Pat the chicken dry with paper towels. Rub it with the olive oil until evenly

coated.

3. In a small bowl, mix together the paprika, garlic, salt, and black pepper and sprinkle it evenly over the chicken.

4. Place the chicken in the prepared basket, breast-side down.

5. Air fry at 360°F (182°C) for 30 minutes, flip, and cook for another 20 minutes, or until the internal temperature reaches 165°F (74°C) and the juices run clear.

6. Sprinkle with the parsley before serving.

Per Serving

Calories: 549 | fat: 11g | protein: 105g | carbs: 0g | fiber: 0g | sodium: 523mg

36. Broccoli Cheese Chicken

Prep time: 10 minutes | Cook time: 19 to 24 minutes | Serves 6

15ml avocado oil

31g chopped onion

63g finely chopped broccoli

113g cream cheese, at room temperature

57g Cheddar cheese, shredded

2g garlic powder

3g sea salt, plus additional for seasoning, divided

0.5g freshly ground black pepper, plus additional for seasoning, divided

907g boneless, skinless chicken breasts

3g smoked paprika

1. Heat a medium skillet over medium-high heat and pour in the avocado oil. Add the onion and broccoli and cook, stirring occasionally, for 5 to 8 minutes, until the onion is tender.

2. Transfer to a large bowl and stir in the cream cheese, Cheddar cheese, and garlic powder, and season to taste with salt and pepper.

3. Hold a sharp knife parallel to the chicken breast and cut a long pocket into one side. Stuff the chicken pockets with the broccoli mixture, using toothpicks to secure the pockets around the filling.

4. In a small dish, combine the paprika, 3g salt, and 0.5g pepper. Sprinkle this over the outside of the chicken.

5. Set the air fryer to 400°F (204°C). Place the chicken in a single layer in the

air fryer basket, cooking in batches if necessary, and cook for 14 to 16 minutes, until an instant-read thermometer reads 160°F (71°C). Place the chicken on a plate and tent a piece of aluminum foil over the chicken. Allow to rest for 5 to 10 minutes before serving.

Per Serving

calorie: 287 | fat: 16g | protein: 32g | carbs: 1g | sugars: 0g | fiber: 0g | sodium: 291mg

37. Chicken Caprese Casserole

Prep time: 10 minutes | Cook time: 6 to 8 hours | Serves 4

907g boneless, skinless chicken thighs, cut into 1-inch cubes

1 (425-g) can no-salt-added diced tomatoes

40g fresh basil leaves (about 1 large bunch)

63ml extra-virgin olive oil

38ml balsamic vinegar

3g sea salt

0.4g freshly ground black pepper

40g shredded mozzarella cheese

1. In a slow cooker, layer the chicken, tomatoes, and basil.
2. In a small bowl, whisk together the olive oil, vinegar, salt, and pepper until blended. Pour the dressing into the slow cooker. Stir to mix well.
3. Cover the cooker and cook for 6 to 8 hours on Low heat.
4. Sprinkle the mozzarella cheese on top. Replace the cover on the cooker and cook for 10 to 20 minutes on Low heat, or until the cheese melts.

Per Serving

Calories: 805 | fat: 61g | protein: 54g | carbs: 8g | fiber: 2g | sodium: 497mg

38. Moroccan-Spiced Chicken Thighs with Saffron Basmati Rice

Prep time: 15 minutes | Cook time: 15 minutes | Serves 2

For the chicken

1.5g paprika

1.5g cumin

1.5g cinnamon

1g salt

1g garlic powder

1g ginger powder

1g coriander

0.5g cayenne pepper (a pinch—or more if you like it spicy)

283g boneless, skinless chicken thighs (about 4 pieces)

For the rice

15ml olive oil

½ small onion, minced

62g basmati rice

2 pinches saffron

1g salt

250ml low-sodium chicken stock

Make the chicken

1. Preheat the oven to 350°F (180°C) and set the rack to the middle position. 2. In a small bowl, combine the paprika, cumin, cinnamon, salt, garlic powder, ginger powder, coriander, and cayenne pepper. Add chicken thighs and toss, rubbing the spice mix into the chicken.

2. Place the chicken in a baking dish and roast it for 35 to 40 minutes, or until the chicken reaches an internal temperature of 165°F(74°C). Let the chicken rest for 5 minutes before serving. Make the rice 1. While the chicken is roasting, heat the oil in a sauté pan over medium-high heat. Add the onion and sauté for 5 minutes.

3. Add the rice, saffron, salt, and chicken stock. Cover the pot with a tight-fitting lid and reduce the heat to low. Let the rice simmer for 15 minutes, or until it is light and fluffy and the liquid has been absorbed.

Per Serving

Calories: 401 | fat: 10g | protein: 37g | carbs: 41g | fiber: 2g | sodium: 715mg

39. Lemon and Paprika Herb-Marinated Chicken

Prep time: 10 minutes | Cook time: 15 minutes | Serves 2

30ml olive oil

60ml freshly squeezed lemon juice

1g salt

2g paprika

1g dried basil

0.5g dried thyme

0.5g garlic powder

2 (113-g) boneless, skinless chicken breasts

1. In a bowl with a lid, combine the olive oil, lemon juice, salt, paprika, basil, thyme, and garlic powder.
2. Add the chicken and marinate for at least 30 minutes, or up to 4 hours.
3. When ready to cook, heat the grill to medium-high and oil the grill grate. Alternately, you can also cook these in a nonstick sauté pan over medium-high heat.
4. Grill the chicken for 6 to 7 minutes, or until it lifts away from the grill easily. Flip it over and grill for another 6 to 7 minutes, or until it reaches an internal temperature of 165°F(74°C).

Per Serving

Calories: 252 | fat: 16g | protein: 27g | carbs: 2g | fiber: 1g | sodium: 372mg

Chapter 5 Fish and Seafood

40. Pecan-Crusted Catfish

Prep time: 5 minutes | Cook time: 12 minutes | Serves 4

60g ground pecans

5g fine sea salt

0.5g ground black pepper

4 (113-g) catfish fillets or haddock fillet

For Garnish (Optional):

Fresh oregano

Pecan halves

1. Spray the air fryer basket with avocado oil. Preheat the air fryer to 375°F (191°C).
2. In a large bowl, mix the pecan meal, salt, and pepper. One at a time, dredge the catfish fillets or haddock fillet in the mixture, coating them well. Use your hands to press the pecan meal into the fillets. Spray the fish with avocado oil and place them in the air fryer basket.

3. Air fry the coated catfish or haddock for 12 minutes, or until it flakes easily and is no longer translucent in the center, flipping halfway through.
4. Garnish with oregano sprigs and pecan halves, if desired.
5. Store leftovers in an airtight container in the fridge for up to 3 days. Reheat in a preheated 350°F (177°C) air fryer for 4 minutes, or until heated through.

Per Serving

Calories: 165 | fat: 3g | protein: 20g | carbs: 12g | fiber: 1g | sodium: 485mg

41. Roasted Mediterranean Fish

Prep time: 10 minutes | Cook time: 35 minutes | Serves 4

350g new potatoes

450g cod fillet

200g cherry tomatoes

1 lemon

15ml olive oil

4 garlic cloves, peeled and crushed

A few sprigs of fresh thyme

Salt and freshly ground black pepper

1. Preheat the oven to 200°C/400°F/Gas 6.
2. Cut the potatoes into bite-sized pieces and place them in a roasting tin.
3. Cut the cod fillet into four equal portions and add them to the roasting tin.
4. Add the cherry tomatoes, lemon, olive oil, garlic and thyme to the tin and season with salt and pepper.
5. Roast for 35 minutes, or until the cod is cooked through and the potatoes are tender.
6. Serve immediately.

Per Serving

Calories: 364|fat: 8.1g|protein: 37.9g |carbs: 28.8g | fiber: 3.3g| sodium: 363mg

42. Italian Breaded Prawns

Prep time: 10 minutes | Cook time: 5 minutes | Serves 4

2 large eggs

250g breadcrumbs

3g Italian seasoning

5g salt

120g flour

454g large prawns (21-25), peeled and deveined

Extra-virgin olive oil

1. In a small bowl, beat the eggs with 15ml water, then transfer to a shallow dish.

2. Add the breadcrumbs and salt to a separate shallow dish; mix well.

3. Place the flour into a third shallow dish.

4. Coat the shrimp in the flour, then egg, and finally the breadcrumbs. Place on a plate and repeat with all of the shrimp.

5. Preheat a skillet over high heat. Pour in enough olive oil to coat the bottom of the skillet. Cook the shrimp in the hot skillet for 2 to 3 minutes on each side. Take the shrimp out and drain on a paper towel. Serve warm.

Per Serving

Calories: 459 | fat: 6g | protein: 36g | carbs: 63g | fiber: 3g | sodium: 617mg

43.Mediterranean Fish And Chorizo Stew

Prep time: 10 minutes | Cook time: 30 minutes | Serves 4

15ml olive oil

0.6g chorizo, diced

0.9g onion, diced

4 garlic cloves, peeled and crushed

30g tomato paste

800g canned diced tomatoes

0.9g green bell pepper, diced

450g white fish fillets, cut into bite-sized pieces

200g clams, scrubbed

200g mussels, scrubbed and debearded

Salt and freshly ground black pepper

1.Heat the oil in a large saucepan over medium heat. Add the chorizo and fry for 2-3 minutes.

2.Add the onion, garlic and tomato paste and fry for a further 2-3 minutes.

3. Add the canned tomatoes and bell pepper and bring to a boil.
4. Add the fish fillets and shellfish and season with salt and pepper.
5. Cook for 3-4 minutes, or until the fish is cooked through and the shellfish have opened.
6. Serve immediately with crusty bread, if desired.

Per Serving

Calories: 401 | fat: 17.1g | protein: 40.5g | carbs: 22.9g | fiber: 5.1g | sodium: 1060mg

44. Baked Salmon with Lemon And Dill

Prep time: 5 minutes | Cook time: 15 minutes | Serves 4

4 salmon fillets, about 0.9g each
0.6g lemon, thinly sliced
2 tablespoons chopped fresh dill
Salt and freshly ground black pepper
Olive oil, for drizzling
Lemon wedges, to serve

1. Preheat the oven to 200° C/400° F/Gas 6.
2. Place the salmon fillets on a baking sheet and top with the lemon slices and chopped dill. Season with salt and pepper.
3. Drizzle with olive oil and bake for 15 minutes, or until the salmon is cooked through.
4. Serve immediately with lemon wedges, if desired.

Per Serving

Calories: 239 | fat: 13.5g | potein: 23.2g | carbs: 0g | fiber: 0g | sodium: 85mg

45. Moroccan Braised Halibut with Cinnamon and Capers

Prep time: 5 minutes | Cook time: 20 minutes | Serves 4

62ml olive oil
1g ground cumin
1 (425g) can diced tomatoes, drained
11g drained capers
2g cinnamon

3g salt, divided

1g freshly ground black pepper, divided

4 halibut fillets, about 170 g each and 1-inch-thick

1. Heat the olive oil in a large skillet over medium heat. Add the cumin and cook, stirring, for 1 minute. Add the tomatoes, capers, cinnamon, 1g salt, and 0.5g pepper and cook for about 10 minutes, until the mixture is thickened.
2. Dry the fish well with paper towels and then season all over with the remaining 1g salt and 0.5g pepper. Add the fish to the sauce in the pan, cover, and simmer for 8 to 10 minutes, until the fish is cooked through. Serve immediately.

Per Serving

Calories: 309 | fat: 14g | protein: 40g | carbs: 5g | fiber: 2g | sodium: 525mg

46. Catfish in Creole Sauce

Prep time: 10 minutes | Cook time: 5 minutes | Serves 4

1 (680g) catfish fillet or haddock fillet , rinsed in cold water, patted dry, cut into bite-sized pieces

1 (411-g) can diced tomatoes

2g dried minced onion

0.5g onion powder

2g dried minced garlic

0.5g garlic powder

2g hot paprika

0.3g dried tarragon

1 medium green bell pepper, seeded and diced

1 stalk celery, finely diced

1g sugar

10g chili sauce

3g salt

1g ground black pepper

1. Add all ingredients to the Instant Pot® and stir to mix.
2. Close lid, set steam release to Sealing, press the Manual button, and set time to 5 minutes. When the timer beeps, quick-release the pressure until the float valve drops and open lid. Gently stir and serve.

Per Serving

Calories: 284 | fat: 9g | protein: 31g | carbs: 7g | fiber: 3g | sodium: 696mg

47. Asian Swordfish

Prep time: 10 minutes | Cook time: 6 to 11 minutes | Serves 4

4 (113g) swordfish steaks

3ml toasted sesame oil

1 jalapeño pepper, finely minced

2 garlic cloves, grated

15g grated fresh ginger

0.5g Chinese five-spice powder

0.5g freshly ground black pepper

30ml freshly squeezed lemon juice

1. Place the swordfish steaks on a work surface and drizzle with the sesame oil.
2. In a small bowl, mix the jalapeño, garlic, ginger, five-spice powder, pepper, and lemon juice. Rub this mixture into the fish and let it stand for 10 minutes.
3. Roast the swordfish in the air fryer at 380°F (193°C) for 6 to 11 minutes, or until the swordfish reaches an internal temperature of at least 140°F (60°C) on a meat thermometer. Serve immediately.

Per Serving

Calories: 175 | fat: 8g | protein: 22g | carbs: 2g | fiber: 0g | sodium: 93mg

48. Cod with Parsley Pistou

Prep time: 15 minutes | Cook time: 10 minutes | Serves 4

120g packed roughly chopped fresh flat-leaf Italian parsley

1 to 2 small garlic cloves, minced

Zest and juice of 1 lemon

5g salt

1g freshly ground black pepper

250ml extra-virgin olive oil, divided

454g cod fillets, cut into 4 equal-sized pieces

1. In a food processer, combine the parsley, garlic, lemon zest and juice, salt, and pepper. Pulse to chop well.

2. While the food processor is running, slowly stream in 188ml olive oil until well combined. Set aside.

3. In a large skillet, heat the remaining 62ml olive oil over medium-high heat. Add the cod fillets, cover, and cook 4 to 5 minutes on each side, or until cooked through. Thicker fillets may require a bit more cooking time. Remove from the heat and keep warm.

4. Add the pistou to the skillet and heat over medium-low heat. Return the cooked fish to the skillet, flipping to coat in the sauce. Serve warm, covered with pistou.

Per Serving

Calories: 580 | fat: 55g | protein: 21g | carbs: 2g | fiber: 1g | sodium: 591mg

49. Seafood Paella

Prep time: 20 minutes | Cook time: 13 minutes | Serves 4

0.5g saffron threads

500ml vegetable stock

30ml olive oil

1 medium yellow onion, peeled and diced

125g diced carrot

1 medium green bell pepper, seeded and diced

125g fresh or frozen green peas

2 cloves garlic, peeled and minced

125g basmati rice

30g chopped fresh flat-leaf parsley

227g medium prawns, peeled and deveined

227g mussels, scrubbed and beards removed

227g clams, rinsed

0.5g ground black pepper

1. Add saffron and broth to a medium microwave-safe bowl and stir well. Microwave for 30 seconds on High to just warm broth. Set aside.

2. Press the Sauté button on the Instant Pot® and heat oil. Add onion, carrot, bell pepper, and peas, and cook until they begin to soften, about 5 minutes. Add garlic and rice. Stir until well coated. Add saffron broth and parsley. Press the Cancel button.

3. Close lid, set steam release to Sealing, press the Manual button, and set time to 7 minutes. When the timer beeps, quick-release the pressure until the float valve drops and open lid. Press the Cancel button.

4. Stir rice mixture, then top with shrimp, mussels, and clams. Close lid, set steam release to Sealing, press the Manual button, and set time to 1 minute. When the timer beeps, let pressure release naturally for 10 minutes. Quick-release the remaining pressure until the float valve drops and open lid. Discard any mussels that haven't opened. Season with black pepper before serving.

Per Serving
Calories: 434 | fat: 11g | protein: 33g | carbs: 52g | fiber: 5g | sodium: 633mg

50. Grilled Salmon

Prep time: 5 minutes | Cook time: 10 minutes | Serves 4

1g garlic powder

1g onion powder

2g freshly ground black pepper

3g salt

4 (142 to 170g) salmon fillets with skin on

62ml lemon juice

1. In a small bowl, mix together the garlic powder, onion powder, black pepper, and salt.
2. Put the salmon in a large dish; pour the lemon juice over the salmon.
3. Season the salmon with the seasoning mix.
4. Preheat a grill, grill pan, or lightly oiled skillet to high heat. Place the salmon on the grill or skillet, skin-side down first.
5. Cook each side for 4 minutes. Serve immediately.

Per Serving
Calories: 238 | fat: 13g | protein: 29g | carbs: 4g | fiber: 0g | sodium: 360mg

51. Grilled Prawns Skewers with Zucchini And Bell Peppers

Prep time: 10 minutes | Cook time: 10 minutes | Serves 4

15ml olive oil, plus extra for drizzling

0.9g onion, diced

3 garlic cloves, peeled and crushed
2.6g dried oregano
0.6g red bell pepper, diced
0.3g yellow bell pepper, diced
250g large prawns, peeled and deveined
150g zucchini, cut into bite-sized pieces
Salt and freshly ground black pepper
Lemon wedges, to serve

1. Heat the oil in a large saucepan over medium heat. Add the onion, garlic and oregano and fry for 2-3 minutes.
2. Add the bell peppers and fry for a further 2-3 minutes.
3. Thread the shrimp and zucchini onto skewers and season with salt and pepper.
4. Grill the skewers for 5-6 minutes, or until the shrimp are cooked through.
5. Drizzle with olive oil and serve immediately with lemon wedges, if desired.

Per Serving
Calories: 107 | fat: 5.4g | protein: 11.7g | carbs: 4.7g | fiber: 1.1g | sodium: 239mg

52. Citrus Mediterranean Salmon with Lemon Caper Sauce
Prep time: 15 minutes | Cook time: 22 minutes | Serves 2

30ml fresh lemon juice
83ml orange juice
15ml extra virgin olive oil
0.5g freshly ground black pepper
2 (170-g) salmon fillets
Lemon Caper Sauce:
30ml extra virgin olive oil
15g finely chopped red onion
1 garlic clove, minced
30ml fresh lemon juice
142g dry white wine
6g capers, rinsed
0.3g freshly ground black pepper

1. Preheat the oven to 350°F (180°C).
2. In a small bowl, combine the lemon juice, orange juice, olive oil, and black

pepper. Whisk until blended, then pour the mixture into a zipper-lock bag. Place the fillets in the bag, shake gently, and transfer the salmon to the refrigerator to marinate for 10 minutes.

3. When the salmon is done marinating, transfer the fillets and marinade to a medium baking dish. Bake for 10–15 minutes or until the salmon is cooked through and the internal temperature reaches 165°F (74°C). Remove the salmon from the oven and cover loosely with foil. Set aside to rest.

4. While the salmon is resting, make the lemon caper sauce by heating the olive oil in a medium pan over medium heat. When the olive oil begins to shimmer, add the onions and sauté for 3 minutes, stirring frequently, then add the garlic and sauté for another 30 seconds.

5. Add the lemon juice and wine. Bring the mixture to a boil and cook until the sauce becomes thick, about 2–3 minutes, then remove the pan from the heat. Add the capers and black pepper, and stir.

6. Transfer the fillets to 2 plates, and spoon 22g the sauce over each fillet. Store covered in the refrigerator for up to 3 days.

Per Serving

Calories: 485 | fat: 28g | protein: 36g | carbs: 11g | fiber: 1g | sodium: 331mg

53. Lemon Salmon with Dill

Prep time: 10 minutes | Cook time: 3 minutes | Serves 4

250ml water
4 (113g) skin-on salmon fillets
3g salt
1g ground black pepper
12g chopped fresh dill
1 small lemon, thinly sliced
30ml extra-virgin olive oil
4g chopped fresh parsley

1. Add water to the Instant Pot® and place rack inside.
2. Season fish fillets with salt and pepper. Place fillets on rack. Top each fillet with dill and two or three lemon slices. Close lid, set steam release to Sealing, press the Steam button, and set time to 3 minutes.
3. When the timer beeps, quick-release the pressure until the float valve drops. Press the Cancel button and open lid. Place fillets on a serving platter, drizzle with olive oil, and garnish with parsley. Serve immediately.

Per Serving

Calories: 160 | fat: 9g | protein: 19g | carbs: 0g | fiber: 0g | sodium: 545mg

Chapter 6 Desserts

54. Cholesterol Caring Nut Clusters

Prep time: 5 minutes | Cook time: 20 minutes | Makes 18 mini clusters

Cluster Base:

125g macadamia nuts

125g pecan halves

62g pistachios

65g tahini or 24g coconut butter (although tahini is preferable)

1 large egg

1g vanilla powder

2g cinnamon

Topping:

57g dark chocolate

15ml virgin coconut oil or 15g cacao butter

Pinch of flaked salt

1. Preheat the oven to 285°F (140°C) fan assisted or 320°F (160°C) conventional.
2. Make the cluster base: Roughly chop the nuts or place in a food processor and pulse until chopped but still chunky. Add the remaining base ingredients. Press the "dough" into 18 mini muffin cups and bake for 15 to 20 minutes, until crispy. Remove from the oven and allow to cool completely. Just before adding the chocolate topping, place them in the freezer for 5 to 10 minutes.
3. Meanwhile, make the topping: Melt the dark chocolate and coconut oil in a double boiler, or use a heatproof bowl placed over a small saucepan filled with 250ml water, placed over medium heat. Let cool to room temperature. Alternatively, use a microwave and melt in short 10- to 15-second bursts until melted, stirring in between.
4. Top the cooled clusters with the melted dark chocolate and flaked salt. Store

in a sealed container in the fridge for up to 2 weeks or freeze for up to 3 months.

Per Serving

Calories: 166 | fat: 16g | protein: 2g | carbs: 5g | fiber: 2g | sodium: 5mg

55. Lemon Fool

Prep time: 25minutes |Cook time: 5 minutes| Serves: 4

250g 2% plain Greek yogurt

1 medium lemon

60ml cold water

5g cornflour

52g honey, divided

166g double cream

Fresh fruit and mint leaves, for serving (optional)

1. Place a large glass bowl and the metal beaters from your electric mixer in the refrigerator to chill. Add the yogurt to a medium glass bowl, and place that bowl in the refrigerator to chill as well.
2. Using a Microplane or citrus zester, zest the lemon into a medium, microwave-safe bowl. Halve the lemon, and squeeze 15ml lemon juice into the bowl. Add the water and cornstarch, and stir well. Whisk in 36g honey. Microwave the lemon mixture on high for 1 minute; stir and microwave for an additional 10 to 30 seconds, until the mixture is thick and bubbling.
3. Remove the bowl of yogurt from the refrigerator, and whisk in the warm lemon mixture. Place the yogurt back in the refrigerator.
4. Remove the large chilled bowl and the beaters from the refrigerator. Assemble your electric mixer with the chilled beaters. Pour the cream into the chilled bowl, and beat until soft peaks form—1 to 3 minutes, depending on the freshness of your cream.
5. Take the chilled yogurt mixture out of the refrigerator. Gently fold it into the whipped cream using a rubber scraper; lift and turn the mixture to prevent the cream from deflating. Chill until serving, at least 15 minutes but no longer than 1 hour.
6. To serve, spoon the lemon fool into four glasses or dessert dishes and drizzle with the remaining 16g honey. Top with fresh fruit and mint, if desired.

Per Serving

Calories: 172 | fat: 8g | protein: 4g | carbs: 22g | fiber: 1g | sodium: 52mg

56. Almond Cookies

Prep time: 5 minutes | Cook time: 10 minutes | Serves 4 to 6

62g sugar

120g (1 stick) room temperature salted butter

1 large egg

188g plain flour

124g ground almonds or almond flour

1. Preheat the oven to 375°F(190°C).
2. Using a mixer, cream together the sugar and butter.
3. Add the egg and mix until combined.
4. Alternately add 62g the flour and ground almonds, at a time, while the mixer is on slow.
5. Once everything is combined, line a baking sheet with parchment paper. Drop 15g dough on the baking sheet, keeping the cookies at least 2 inches apart.
6. Put the baking sheet in the oven and bake just until the cookies start to turn brown around the edges, about 5 to 7 minutes.

Per Serving

Calories: 604 | fat: 36g | protein: 11g | carbs: 63g | fiber: 4g | sodium: 181mg

57. Minty Cantaloupe Granita

Prep time: 10 minutes | Cook time: 5 minutes | Serves 4

92g honey

62ml water

6g fresh mint leaves, plus more for garnish

1 medium cantaloupe (about 1.8 kg) peeled, seeded, and cut into 1-inch chunks

1. In a small saucepan set over low heat, combine the honey and water and cook, stirring, until the honey has fully dissolved. Stir in the mint and remove from the heat. Set aside to cool.
2. In a food processor, process the cantaloupe until very smooth. Transfer to a

medium bowl. Remove the mint leaves from the syrup and discard them. Pour the syrup into the cantaloupe purée and stir to mix.

3. Transfer the mixture into a 7-by-12-inch glass baking dish and freeze, stirring with a fork every 30 minutes, for 3 to 4 hours, until it is frozen, but still grainy. Serve chilled, scooped into glasses and garnished with mint leaves.

Per Serving

Calories: 174 | fat: 0g | protein: 1g | carbs: 47g | fiber: 1g | sodium: 9mg

58. Golden Coconut Cream Pops

Prep time: 5 minutes | Cook time: 0 minutes | Makes 8 cream pops

375ml coconut cream

125ml coconut milk

4 egg yolks

6g ground turmeric

3g ground ginger

3g cinnamon

1g vanilla powder or 3g unsweetened vanilla extract

0.5g ground black pepper

Optional: low-carb sweetener, to taste

1. Place all of the ingredients in a blender (including the optional sweetener) and process until well combined. Pour into eight 80 ml ice pop molds. Freeze until solid for 3 hours, or until set.

2. To easily remove the ice pops from the molds, fill a pot as tall as the ice pops with warm (not hot) water and dip the ice pop molds in for 15 to 20 seconds. Remove the ice pops from the molds and then freeze again. Store in the freezer in a resealable bag for up to 3 months.

Per Serving

Calories: 219 | fat: 21g | protein: 3g | carbs: 5g | fiber: 2g | sodium: 9mg

59. Light and Lemony Olive Oil Cupcakes

Prep time: 10 minutes | Cook time: 24 minutes | Serves 18

250g plain flour

20g baking powder
200g granulated sugar
250ml extra virgin olive oil
2 eggs
198g 2% Greek yogurt
1g pure vanilla extract
60ml fresh lemon juice
Zest of 2 lemons
Glaze:
15ml lemon juice
75g icing sugar

1. Preheat the oven to 350°F (180°C). Line a 12-cup muffin pan with cupcake liners and then line a second pan with 6 liners. Set aside.
2. In a medium bowl, combine the flour and baking powder. Whisk and set aside.
3. In a large bowl, combine the sugar and olive oil, and mix until smooth. Add the eggs, one at a time, and mix well. Add the Greek yogurt, vanilla extract, lemon juice, and lemon zest. Mix until well combined.
4. Add the flour mixture to 60g the batter, at a time, while continuously mixing.
5. Spoon the batter into the liners, filling each liner two-thirds full. Bake for 22–25 minutes or until a toothpick inserted into the center of a cupcake comes out clean.
6. While the cupcakes are baking, make the glaze by combining the lemon juice and powdered sugar in a small bowl. Stir until smooth, then set aside.
7. Set the cupcakes aside to cool in the pans for about 5 minutes, then remove the cupcakes from the pans and transfer to a wire rack to cool completely.
8. Drizzle the glaze over the cooled cupcakes. Store in the refrigerator for up to 4 days.

Per Serving
Calories: 225 | fat: 13g | protein: 3g | carbs: 25g | fiber: 1g | sodium: 13mg

60. Blueberry Panna Cotta

Prep time: 5 minutes | Cook time: 0 minutes | Serves 6

9g gelatin powder

30ml water

500g goat's cream, coconut cream, or double cream

250g wild blueberries, fresh or frozen, divided

3g vanilla powder or 7g unsweetened vanilla extract

Optional: low-carb sweetener, to taste

1. In a bowl, sprinkle the gelatin powder over the cold water. Set aside to let it bloom.
2. Place the goat's cream, half of the blueberries, and the vanilla in a blender and process until smooth and creamy. Alternatively, use an immersion blender.
3. Pour the blueberry cream into a saucepan. Gently heat; do not boil. Scrape the gelatin into the hot cream mixture together with the sweetener, if using. Mix well until all the gelatin has dissolved.
4. Divide among 6 (113-g) jars or serving glasses and fill them about two-thirds full, leaving enough space for the remaining blueberries. Place in the fridge for 3 to 4 hours, or until set.
5. When the panna cotta has set, evenly distribute the remaining blueberries among the jars. Serve immediately or store in the fridge for up to 4 days.

Per Serving

Calories: 172 | fat: 15g | protein: 2g | carbs: 8g | fiber: 2g | sodium: 19mg

61. Cocoa and Coconut Banana Slices

Prep time: 10 minutes | Cook time: 0 minutes | Serves 1

1 banana, peeled and sliced

10g unsweetened, shredded coconut

7g unsweetened cocoa powder

5g honey

1. Lay the banana slices on a parchment-lined baking sheet in a single layer. Put in the freezer for about 10 minutes, until firm but not frozen solid. Mix the coconut with the cocoa powder in a small bowl.

2. Roll the banana slices in honey, followed by the coconut mixture.

3. You can either eat immediately or put back in the freezer for a frozen, sweet treat.

Per Serving

Calories: 187 | fat: 4g | protein: 3g | carbs: 41g | fiber: 6g | sodium: 33mg

62. Chocolate Hazelnut "Powerhouse" Truffles

Prep time: 5 minutes | Cook time: 50 minutes | Makes 12 truffles

Filling:

216g blanched hazelnuts, divided

125g coconut butter

72g butter or 63ml virgin coconut oil

31g collagen powder

30g raw cacao powder

2g vanilla powder or cinnamon

Optional: low-carb sweetener, to taste

Chocolate Coating:

71g 100% dark chocolate

28g cacao butter

Pinch of salt

1. Preheat the oven to 285°F (140°C) fan assisted or 320°F (160°C) conventional.

2. To make the filling: Spread the hazelnuts on a baking tray and roast for 40 to 50 minutes, until lightly golden. Remove from the oven and let cool for a few minutes.

3. Place 125g the roasted hazelnuts in a food processor. Process for 1 to 2 minutes, until chunky. Add the coconut butter, butter, collagen powder, cacao powder, vanilla, and sweetener, if using. Process again until well combined. Place the dough in the fridge to set for 1 hour.

4. Reserve 12 hazelnuts for filling and crumble the remaining hazelnuts unto small pieces.

5. To make the chocolate coating: Line a baking tray with parchment. Melt the dark chocolate and cacao butter in a double boiler, or use a heatproof bowl placed over a small saucepan filled with 250ml water, placed over medium heat.

Remove from the heat and let cool to room temperature before using for coating. Alternatively, use a microwave and melt in short 10- to 15-second bursts until melted, stirring in between.

6. Remove the dough from the fridge and use a spoon to scoop about 28 g of the dough. Press one whole hazelnut into the center and use your hands to wrap the dough around to create a truffle. Place in the freezer for about 15 minutes.

7. Gently pierce each very cold truffle with a toothpick or a fork. Working one at a time, hold the truffle over the melted chocolate and spoon the chocolate over it to coat completely. Turn the toothpick as you work until the coating is solidified. Place the coated truffles on the lined tray and drizzle any remaining coating over them. Before they become completely solid, roll them in the chopped nuts. Refrigerate the coated truffles for at least 15 minutes to harden.

8. Keep refrigerated for up to 1 week or freeze for up to 3 months.

Per Serving

Calories: 231 | fat: 22g | protein: 4g | carbs: 8g | fiber: 4g | sodium: 3mg

63. Apple and Brown Rice Pudding

Prep time: 10 minutes | Cook time: 20 minutes | Serves 6

500ml almond milk

125g long-grain brown rice

62g golden raisins

1 Granny Smith apple, peeled, cored, and chopped

31g honey

4g vanilla extract

1g ground cinnamon

1. Place all ingredients in the Instant Pot®. Stir to combine. Close lid, set steam release to Sealing, press the Manual button, and set time to 20 minutes.

2. When the timer beeps, let pressure release naturally for 15 minutes, then quick-release the remaining pressure. Press the Cancel button and open lid. Serve warm or at room temperature.

Per Serving

Calories: 218 | fat: 2g | protein: 3g | carbs: 51g | fiber: 4g | sodium: 54mg

64. Strawberry-Pomegranate Molasses Sauce

Prep time: 10 minutes | Cook time: 5 minutes | Serves 6

45ml olive oil

31g honey

2 pints strawberries, hulled and halved

15 to 30g pomegranate molasses

6g chopped fresh mint

Greek yogurt, for serving

1. In a medium saucepan, heat the olive oil over medium heat. Add the strawberries; cook until their juices are released. Stir in the honey and cook for 1 to 2 minutes. Stir in the molasses and mint. Serve warm over Greek yogurt.

Per Serving

Calories: 189 | fat: 7g | protein: 4g | carbs: 24g | fiber: 3g | sodium: 12mg

65. Nut Butter Cup Fat Bomb

Prep time: 5 minutes | Cook time: 0 minutes | Serves 8

125g crunchy almond butter (no sugar added)

125ml light fruity extra-virgin olive oil

33g ground flaxseed

15g unsweetened cocoa powder

4g vanilla extract

3g ground cinnamon (optional)

5 to 10g sugar-free sweetener of choice (optional)

1. In a mixing bowl, combine the almond butter, olive oil, flaxseed, cocoa powder, vanilla, cinnamon (if using), and sweetener (if using) and stir well with a spatula to combine. Mixture will be a thick liquid.
2. Pour into 8 mini muffin liners and freeze until solid, at least 12 hours. Store in the freezer to maintain their shape.

Per Serving

Calories: 239 | fat: 24g | protein: 4g | carbs: 5g | fiber: 3g | sodium: 3mg

66. Creamy Rice Pudding

Prep time: 5 minutes | Cook time: 45 minutes | Serves 6

156g long-grain rice

1250ml whole milk

125g sugar

15ml rose water or orange blossom water

3g cinnamon

1. Rinse the rice under cold water for 30 seconds.
2. Put the rice, milk, and sugar in a large pot. Bring to a gentle boil while continually stirring.
3. Turn the heat down to low and let simmer for 40 to 45 minutes, stirring every 3 to 4 minutes so that the rice does not stick to the bottom of the pot.
4. Add the rose water at the end and simmer for 5 minutes.
5. Divide the pudding into 6 bowls. Sprinkle the top with cinnamon. Cool for at least 1 hour before serving. Store in the fridge.

Per Serving

Calories: 394 | fat: 7g | protein: 9g | carbs: 75g | fiber: 1g | sodium: 102mg

67. Greek Yogurt Chocolate "Mousse" with Berries

Prep time: 15 minutes | Cook time: 0 minutes | Serves 4

560g plain Greek yogurt

62g double cream

63ml pure maple syrup

21g unsweetened cocoa powder

5g vanilla extract

1g coarse sea salt

125g fresh mixed berries

62g chocolate chips

1. Place the yogurt, cream, maple syrup, cocoa powder, vanilla, and salt in the bowl of a stand mixer or use a large bowl with an electric hand mixer. Mix at medium-high speed until fluffy, about 5 minutes.
2. Spoon evenly among 4 bowls and put in the refrigerator to set for at least 15 minutes.
3. Serve each bowl with 62g mixed berries and 15g chocolate chips.

Per Serving

Calories: 300 | fat: 11g | protein: 16g | carbs: 35g | fiber: 3g | sodium: 60mg

Chapter 7 Snacks and Appetizers

68. Roasted Chickpeas with Herbs and Spices

Prep time: 5 minutes | Cook time: 22 minutes | Serves 4

1 (425-g) can chickpeas, drained and rinsed

15ml olive oil

1g za'atar

1g ground sumac

2g Aleppo pepper

5g brown sugar

3g coarse sea salt

8g chopped fresh parsley

1. Preheat the oven to 350°F (180°C).
2. Spread the chickpeas in an even layer on an ungreased rimmed baking sheet and bake for 10 minutes, or until they are dried. Remove from the oven; keep the oven on.
3. Meanwhile, in a medium bowl, whisk together the olive oil, za'atar, sumac, Aleppo pepper, brown sugar, and salt until well combined.
4. Add the warm chickpeas to the oil-spice mixture and stir until they are completely coated. Return the chickpeas to the baking sheet and spread them into an even layer. Bake for 10 to 12 minutes more, until fragrant.
5. Transfer the chickpeas to a serving bowl, toss with the parsley, and serve.

Per Serving

Calories: 122 | fat: 5g | protein: 5g | carbs: 16g | fiber: 4g | sodium: 427mg

69. Lemon Prawns with Garlic Olive Oil

Prep time: 5 minutes | Cook time: 6 minutes | Serves 4

454g medium prawns, cleaned and deveined

92ml olive oil, divided
Juice of ½ lemon
3 garlic cloves, minced and divided
3g salt
1g red pepper flakes
Lemon wedges, for serving (optional)
Ready-made tomato sauce, for dipping (optional)

1. Preheat the air fryer to 380°F(193°C).
2. In a large bowl, combine the shrimp with 30ml the olive oil, as well as the lemon juice, ⅓ of the minced garlic, salt, and red pepper flakes. Toss to coat the shrimp well.
3. In a small ramekin, combine the remaining 62ml olive oil and the remaining minced garlic.
4. Tear off a 12-by-12-inch sheet of aluminum foil. Pour the shrimp into the center of the foil, then fold the sides up and crimp the edges so that it forms an aluminum foil bowl that is open on top. Place this packet into the air fryer basket.
5. Roast the shrimp for 4 minutes, then open the air fryer and place the ramekin with oil and garlic in the basket beside the shrimp packet. Cook for 2 more minutes.
6. Transfer the shrimp on a serving plate or platter with the ramekin of garlic olive oil on the side for dipping. You may also serve with lemon wedges and marinara sauce, if desired.

Per Serving
Calories: 283 | fat: 21g | protein: 23g | carbs: 1g | fiber: 0g | sodium: 427mg

70. Mixed-Vegetable Caponata
Prep time: 15 minutes | Cook time: 40 minutes | Serves 8
1 aubergine, chopped
1 courgette, chopped
1 red bell pepper, seeded and chopped
1 small red onion, chopped
30ml extra-virgin olive oil, divided

250g canned tomato sauce

45ml red wine vinegar

20g honey

1g red-pepper flakes

1g coarse sea salt

62g pitted, chopped green olives

30g drained capers

30g raisins

30g chopped fresh flat-leaf parsley

1. Preheat the oven to 400°F(205°C).
2. On a large rimmed baking sheet, toss the eggplant, zucchini, bell pepper, and onion with 15ml oil. Roast until the vegetables are tender, about 30 minutes.
3. In a medium saucepan over medium heat, warm the remaining 15ml oil. Add the tomato sauce, vinegar, honey, pepper flakes, and salt and stir to combine. Add the roasted vegetables, olives, capers, raisins, and parsley and cook until bubbly and thickened, 10 minutes.
4. Remove from the heat and cool to room temperature. Serve immediately or store in an airtight container in the refrigerator for up to 1 week.

Per Serving

Calories: 100 | fat: 5g | protein: 2g | carbs: 13g | fiber: 4g | sodium: 464mg

71. Five-Ingredient Falafel with Garlic-Yogurt Sauce

Prep time: 5 minutes | Cook time: 15 minutes | Serves 4

Falafel:

1 (425-g) can chickpeas, drained and rinsed

31g fresh parsley

2 garlic cloves, minced

7g ground cumin

15g wholemeal flour

3g Salt

Garlic-Yogurt Sauce:

250g nonfat plain Greek yogurt

1 garlic clove, minced

3g chopped fresh dill

30ml lemon juice

Make the Falafel:

1. Preheat the air fryer to 360°F(182°C).
2. Put the chickpeas into a food processor. Pulse until mostly chopped, then add the parsley, garlic, and cumin and pulse for another 1 to 2 minutes, or until the ingredients are combined and turning into a dough.
3. Add the flour. Pulse a few more times until combined. The dough will have texture, but the chickpeas should be pulsed into small bits.
4. Using clean hands, roll the dough into 8 balls of equal size, then pat the balls down a bit so they are about ½-thick disks.
5. Spray the basket of the air fryer with olive oil cooking spray, then place the falafel patties in the basket in a single layer, making sure they don't touch each other.
6. Fry in the air fryer for 15 minutes. Make the garlic-yogurt sauce
7. In a small bowl, combine the yogurt, garlic, dill, and lemon juice.
8. Once the falafel are done cooking and nicely browned on all sides, remove them from the air fryer and season with salt.
9. Serve hot with a side of dipping sauce.

Per Serving

Calories: 150 | fat: 3g | protein: 10g | carbs: 23g | fiber: 6g | sodium: 194mg

72. Zucchini Feta Roulades

Prep time: 10 minutes | Cook time: 10 minutes | Serves 6

125g feta

1 garlic clove, minced

6g fresh basil, minced

8g capers, minced

0.5g salt

0.5g red pepper flakes

15ml lemon juice

2 medium courgettes

12 toothpicks

1. Preheat the air fryer to 360°F (182°C).(If using a grill attachment, make sure it is inside the air fryer during preheating.)
2. In a small bowl, combine the feta, garlic, basil, capers, salt, red pepper flakes, and lemon juice.
3. Slice the zucchini into ⅛-inch strips lengthwise. (Each zucchini should yield around 6 strips.)
4. Spread 18g the cheese filling onto each slice of zucchini, then roll it up and secure it with a toothpick through the middle.
5. Place the zucchini roulades into the air fryer basket in a single layer, making sure that they don't touch each other.
6. Bake or grill in the air fryer for 10 minutes.
7. Remove the zucchini roulades from the air fryer and gently remove the toothpicks before serving.

Per Serving

Calories: 36 | fat: 3g | protein: 2g | carbs: 1g | fiber: 0g | sodium: 200mg

73. Parmesan French Fries

Prep time: 10 minutes | Cook time: 25 minutes | Serves 2 to 3

2 to 3 large floury potatoes, peeled and cut into ½-inch sticks

10ml vegetable or canola oil

188g grated Parmesan cheese

3g salt

1g Freshly ground black pepper, to taste

5g fresh chopped parsley

1. Bring a large saucepan of salted water to a boil on the stovetop while you peel and cut the potatoes. Blanch the potatoes in the boiling salted water for 4 minutes while you preheat the air fryer to 400°F (204°C). Strain the potatoes and rinse them with cold water. Dry them well with a clean kitchen towel.
2. Toss the dried potato sticks gently with the oil and place them in the air fryer basket. Air fry for 25 minutes, shaking the basket a few times while the fries cook to help them brown evenly.
3. Combine the Parmesan cheese, salt and pepper. With 2 minutes left on the air fryer cooking time, sprinkle the fries with the Parmesan cheese mixture.

Toss the fries to coat them evenly with the cheese mixture and continue to air fry for the final 2 minutes, until the cheese has melted and just starts to brown. Sprinkle the finished fries with chopped parsley, a little more grated Parmesan cheese if you like, and serve.

Per Serving

Calories: 252 | fat: 11g | protein: 13g | carbs: 27g | fiber: 2g | sodium: 411mg

74. Stuffed Dates with Feta, Parmesan, and Pine Nuts

Prep time: 5 minutes | Cook time: 10 minutes | Serves 4

28 g feta

28g Parmesan cheese

12 dried dates, pitted

8g raw pine nuts

5ml extra virgin olive oil

1. Preheat the oven to 425°F (220°C). Line a small baking pan with parchment paper.
2. Cut the feta and Parmesan into 12 small thin sticks, each about ¾ inch long and ¼ inch thick.
3. Use a sharp knife to cut a small slit lengthwise into each date. Insert a piece of the Parmesan followed by a piece of the feta, and then press 2–3 pine nuts slightly into the feta.
4. Transfer the dates to the prepared baking pan and place in the oven to roast for 10 minutes. (The edges of the dates should begin to brown.)
5. Remove the dates from the oven and drizzle a few drops of the olive oil over each date. Serve promptly. (These do not store well and are best enjoyed fresh.)

Per Serving

Calories: 126 | fat: 5g | protein: 4g | carbs: 17g | fiber: 2g | sodium: 194mg

75.Mediterranean Scones

Prep time: 15 minutes | Cook time: 20 minutes | Serves 5

225g self-raising flour

85g caster sugar

1tsp baking powder

140ml milk

1 egg, beaten

50g butter, melted

Zest of 1 lemon

Juice of ½ lemon

1.Preheat the oven to 200C/400F/Gas 6.

2.Sift the flour, sugar and baking powder into a large bowl. Make a well in the centre and pour in the milk and egg. Gradually mix together until you have a soft dough.

3.Stir in the butter, lemon zest and lemon juice until thoroughly combined.

4.Place spoonfuls of mixture onto a baking sheet and bake for 15-20 minutes until golden brown and well-risen. Serve warm with butter and jam.

Per Serving

Calories: 343 | fat: 10.4g |protein: 6.1g |carbs:54.3g |fiber:1.4g |sodium: 247mg

76. Pesto Cucumber Boats

Prep time: 10 minutes | Cook time: 0 minutes | Serves 4 to 6

3 medium cucumbers

1g salt

20g fresh basil leaves

1 garlic clove, minced

31g walnut pieces

62g grated Parmesan cheese

62ml extra-virgin olive oil

1g paprika

1. Cut each cucumber in half lengthwise and again in half crosswise to make 4 stocky pieces. Use a spoon to remove the seeds and hollow out a shallow trough in each piece. Lightly salt each piece and set aside on a platter.

2. In a blender or food processor, combine the basil, garlic, walnuts, Parmesan cheese, and olive oil and blend until smooth.

3. Use a spoon to spread pesto into each cucumber "boat" and sprinkle each with paprika. Serve.

Per Serving

Calories: 143 | fat: 14g | protein: 3g | carbs: 4g | fiber: 1g | sodium: 175mg

77. Lemony Olives and Feta Medley

Prep time: 10 minutes | Cook time: 0 minutes | Serves 8

1 (454g) block of Greek feta cheese

750ml mixed olives (Kalamata and green), drained from brine; pitted preferred

62ml extra-virgin olive oil

45ml lemon juice

5g grated lemon zest

1g dried oregano

Pita bread, for serving

1. Cut the feta cheese into ½-inch squares and put them into a large bowl.
2. Add the olives to the feta and set aside.
3. In a small bowl, whisk together the olive oil, lemon juice, lemon zest, and oregano.
4. Pour the dressing over the feta cheese and olives and gently toss together to evenly coat everything.
5. Serve with pita bread.

Per Serving

Calories: 269 | fat: 24g | protein: 9g | carbs: 6g | fiber: 2g | sodium: 891mg

78. Bravas-Style Potatoes

Prep time: 15 minutes | Cook time: 50 minutes | Serves 8

4 large russet potatoes (about 1.1 kg), scrubbed and cut into 1' cubes

6g coarse sea salt, divided

1g ground black pepper

1g red-pepper flakes

½ small yellow onion, chopped

1 large tomato, chopped

5ml sherry vinegar

2g hot paprika

15g chopped fresh flat-leaf parsley Hot sauce (optional)

1. Preheat the oven to 450°F(235°C). Bring a large pot of well-salted water to a

boil.

2. Boil the potatoes until just barely tender, 5 to 8 minutes. Drain and transfer the potatoes to a large rimmed baking sheet. Add 15ml the oil, 3g kosher salt, the black pepper, and pepper flakes. With 2 large spoons, toss very well to coat the potatoes in the oil. Spread the potatoes out on the baking sheet. Roast until the bottoms are starting to brown and crisp, 20 minutes. Carefully flip the potatoes and roast until the other side is golden and crisp, 15 to 20 minutes.

3. Meanwhile, in a small skillet over medium heat, warm the remaining 15ml oil. Cook the onion until softened, 3 to 4 minutes. Add the tomato and cook until it's broken down and saucy, 5 minutes. Stir in the vinegar, paprika, and the remaining 3g salt. Cook for 30 seconds, remove from the heat, and cover to keep warm.

4. Transfer the potatoes to a large serving bowl. Drizzle the tomato mixture over the potatoes. Sprinkle with the parsley. Serve with hot sauce, if using.

Per Serving

Calories: 173 | fat: 2g | protein: 4g | carbs: 35g | fiber: 3g | sodium: 251mg

79. Marinated Feta and Artichokes

Prep time: 10 minutes | Cook time: 0 minutes | Makes 375ml

113 g traditional Greek feta, cut into ½-inch cubes

113 g drained artichoke hearts, quartered lengthwise

125ml extra-virgin olive oil

Zest and juice of 1 lemon

8g roughly chopped fresh rosemary

8g roughly chopped fresh parsley

3g black peppercorns

1. In a glass bowl or large glass jar, combine the feta and artichoke hearts. Add the olive oil, lemon zest and juice, rosemary, parsley, and peppercorns and toss gently to coat, being sure not to crumble the feta.

2. Cover and refrigerate for at least 4 hours, or up to 4 days. Pull out of the refrigerator 30 minutes before serving.

Per Serving

Calories: 108 | fat: 9g | protein: 3g | carbs: 4g | fiber: 1g | sodium: 294mg

80. Savory Mackerel & Goat'S Cheese "Paradox" Balls

Prep time: 10 minutes | Cook time: 0 minutes | Makes 10 fat bombs

2 smoked or cooked mackerel fillets, boneless, skin removed

125 g soft goat's cheese

15ml fresh lemon juice

5g Dijon or yellow mustard

1 small red onion, finely diced

6g chopped fresh chives or herbs of choice

94g pecans, crushed

10 leaves baby gem lettuce

1. In a food processor, combine the mackerel, goat's cheese, lemon juice, and mustard. Pulse until smooth. Transfer to a bowl, add the onion and herbs, and mix with a spoon. Refrigerate for 20 to 30 minutes, or until set.

2. Using a large spoon or an ice cream scoop, divide the mixture into 10 balls, about 40g each. Roll each ball in the crushed pecans. Place each ball on a small lettuce leaf and serve. Keep the fat bombs refrigerated in a sealed container for up to 5 days.

Per Serving (1 fat bomb)

Calories: 165 | fat: 12g | protein: 12g | carbs: 2g | fiber: 1g | sodium: 102mg

Chapter 8 Beans and Grains

81. Tomato Rice

Prep time: 10 minutes | Cook time: 25 minutes | Serves 3

30ml extra virgin olive oil

1 medium onion (any variety), chopped

1 garlic clove, finely chopped

125g uncooked medium-grain rice

18g tomato paste

454g canned crushed tomatoes, or 454g fresh tomatoes (puréed in a food processor)

4g fine sea salt
5g granulated sugar
500ml hot water
6g chopped fresh mint or basil

1. Heat the olive oil in a wide, deep pan over medium heat. When the oil begins to shimmer, add the onion and sauté for 3–4 minutes or until soft, then add the garlic and sauté for an additional 30 seconds.
2. Add the rice and stir until the rice is coated with the oil, then add the tomato paste and stir rapidly. Add the tomatoes, sea salt, and sugar, and then stir again.
3. Add the hot water, stir, then reduce the heat to low and simmer, covered, for 20 minutes or until the rice is soft. (If the rice appears to need more cooking time, add a small amount of hot water to the pan and continue cooking.) Remove the pan from the heat.
4. Add the chopped mint or basil, and let the rice sit for 10 minutes before serving. Store covered in the refrigerator for up to 4 days.

Per Serving

Calories: 359 | fat: 11g | protein: 7g | carbs: 60g | fiber: 6g | sodium: 607mg

82. Couscous with Apricots

Prep time: 10 minutes | Cook time: 15 minutes | Serves 4

30ml olive oil
1 small onion, diced
125g whole-wheat couscous
500ml water or stock
62g dried apricots, soaked in water overnight
62g flaked almonds or pistachios
0.5g dried mint
0.5g dried thyme

1. Heat the olive oil in a large skillet over medium-high heat. Add the onion and cook until translucent and soft.
2. Stir in the couscous and cook for 2–3 minutes.
3. Add the water or broth, cover, and cook for 8–10 minutes until the water is mostly absorbed.

4. Remove from the heat and let stand for a few minutes.
5. Fluff with a fork and fold in the apricots, nuts, mint, and thyme.

Per Serving

Calories: 294 | fat: 15g | protein: 8g | carbs: 38g | fiber: 6g | sodium: 6mg

83. Three-Grain Pilaf

Prep time: 10 minutes | Cook time: 10 minutes | Serves 6

30ml extra-virgin olive oil

62g sliced spring onions

125g jasmine rice

62g millet

62g quinoa, rinsed and drained

625ml vegetable stock

1g salt

1g ground black pepper

1. Press the Sauté button on the Instant Pot® and heat oil. Add scallions and cook until just tender, 2 minutes. Add rice, millet, and quinoa and cook for 3 minutes to toast. Add stock and stir well. Press the Cancel button.
2. Close lid, set steam release to Sealing, press the Manual button, and set time to 4 minutes. When the timer beeps, quick-release the pressure until the float valve drops and open the lid. Fluff pilaf with a fork and stir in salt and pepper. Serve warm.

Per Serving

Calories: 346 | fat: 7g | protein: 8g | carbs: 61g | fiber: 4g | sodium: 341mg

84. Garlic Shrimp with Quinoa

Prep time: 10 minutes | Cook time: 30 minutes | Serves 4

1000ml chicken stock

250g uncooked quinoa, rinsed

75ml olive oil

½ red onion, chopped

6 garlic cloves, minced

18g tomato paste

2g chili powder

Sea salt

1g Freshly ground black pepper

680g medium prawns (36/40 count), peeled and deveined

125g crumbled feta cheese, for garnish

1. In a large stockpot, combine the broth and quinoa and bring to a boil over high heat. Reduce the heat to low, cover, and simmer for 20 to 25 minutes, until the quinoa is cooked. Drain the quinoa and set aside in a medium bowl. 2. Rinse and dry the pot. Pour in the olive oil and heat over medium heat. Add the onion, garlic, tomato paste, and chili powder and cook for 1 minute. Season with salt and pepper and stir to combine. Add the shrimp and cook until the shrimp are pink and just cooked through, 5 to 7 minutes.

2. Return the quinoa to the pot and stir everything together. Remove from the heat.

3. Serve topped with the feta.

Per Serving

Calories: 712 | fat: 28g | protein: 54g | carbs: 62g | fiber: 7g | sodium: 474mg

85. Mediterranean Lentils and Rice

Prep time: 5 minutes |Cook time: 25 minutes| Serves: 4

562ml low-sodium or no-salt-added vegetable stock

62g uncooked brown or green lentils

62g uncooked instant brown rice

62g diced carrots (about 1 carrot)

62g diced celery (about 1 stalk)

1 (64g) can sliced olives, drained (about 125ml)

31g diced red onion (about ⅛ onion)

31g chopped fresh curly-leaf parsley

23ml extra-virgin olive oil

15ml freshly squeezed lemon juice (from about ½ small lemon)

1 garlic clove, minced (about 3g)

1g sea salt

0.5g freshly ground black pepper

1. In a medium saucepan over high heat, bring the broth and lentils to a boil,

cover, and lower the heat to medium-low. Cook for 8 minutes.

2. Raise the heat to medium, and stir in the rice. Cover the pot and cook the mixture for 15 minutes, or until the liquid is absorbed. Remove the pot from the heat and let it sit, covered, for 1 minute, then stir.

3. While the lentils and rice are cooking, mix together the carrots, celery, olives, onion, and parsley in a large serving bowl.

4. In a small bowl, whisk together the oil, lemon juice, garlic, salt, and pepper. Set aside.

5. When the lentils and rice are cooked, add them to the serving bowl. Pour the dressing on top, and mix everything together. Serve warm or cold, or store in a sealed container in the refrigerator for up to 7 days.

Per Serving

Calories: 183 | fat: 6g | protein:5g | carbs: 29.5g | fiber: 3.3g | sodium: 552mg

86. Lentil and Zucchini Boats

Prep time: 15 minutes | Cook time: 50 minutes | Serves 4

125g dried green lentils, rinsed and drained

1g salt

500ml water

15ml olive oil

½ medium red onion, peeled and diced

1 clove garlic, peeled and minced

225g ready-made tomato sauce

1g crushed red pepper flakes

4 medium courgettes, trimmed and cut lengthwise

63g shredded part-skim mozzarella cheese

31g chopped fresh flat-leaf parsley

1. Add lentils, salt, and water to the Instant Pot®. Close lid, set steam release to Sealing, press the Manual button, and set time to 12 minutes. When the timer beeps, quick-release the pressure until the float valve drops. Press the Cancel button. Open lid and drain off any excess liquid. Transfer lentils to a medium bowl. Set aside.

2. Press the Sauté button and heat oil. Add onion and cook until tender, about

3 minutes. Add garlic and cook until fragrant, about 30 seconds. Add marinara sauce and crushed red pepper flakes and stir to combine. Press the Cancel button. Stir in lentils.

3. Preheat oven to 350°F (180°C) and spray a 9" × 13" baking dish with nonstick cooking spray.

4. Using a teaspoon, hollow out each zucchini half. Lay zucchini in prepared baking dish. Divide lentil mixture among prepared zucchini. Top with cheese. Bake for 30–35 minutes, or until zucchini are tender and cheese is melted and browned. Top with parsley and serve hot.

Per Serving

Calories: 326 | fat: 10g | protein: 22g | carbs: 39g | fiber: 16g | sodium: 568mg

87. Greek Chickpeas with Coriander and Sage

Prep time: 20 minutes | Cook time: 22 minutes | Serves 6 to 8

8g table salt, for brining

454g dried chickpeas, picked over and rinsed

30ml extra-virgin olive oil, plus extra for drizzling

2 onions, halved and sliced thin

1g table salt

5g coriander seeds, cracked

1–3g red pepper flakes

312g chicken stock

17g fresh sage leaves

2 bay leaves

8g grated lemon zest plus 10ml juice

8g minced fresh parsley

1. Dissolve 7g salt in 2 quarts cold water in large container. Add chickpeas and soak at room temperature for at least 8 hours or up to 24 hours. Drain and rinse well.

2. Using highest sauté function, heat oil in Instant Pot until shimmering. Add onions and 1g salt and cook until onions are softened and well browned, 10 to 12 minutes. Stir in coriander and pepper flakes and cook until fragrant, about 30 seconds. Stir in broth, scraping up any browned bits, then stir in chickpeas,

sage, and bay leaves.

3. Lock lid in place and close pressure release valve. Select low pressure cook function and cook for 10 minutes. Turn off Instant Pot and let pressure release naturally for 15 minutes. Quick-release any remaining pressure, then carefully remove lid, allowing steam to escape away from you.

4. Discard bay leaves. Stir lemon zest and juice into chickpeas and season with salt and pepper to taste. Sprinkle with parsley. Serve, drizzling individual portions with extra oil.

Per Serving

Calories: 190 | fat: 6g | protein: 11g | carbs: 40g | fiber: 1g | sodium: 360mg

88. Giant Beans with Tomato and Parsley

Prep time: 10 minutes | Cook time: 54 minutes | Serves 8

30ml light olive oil

1 medium white onion, peeled and chopped

2 cloves garlic, peeled and minced

454g dried giant beans, soaked overnight and drained

2 thyme sprigs

1 bay leaf

1250ml water

1 (425g) can diced tomatoes, drained

1 (227g) can tomato sauce

31g chopped fresh flat-leaf parsley

7g chopped fresh oregano

3g chopped fresh dill

126g crumbled feta cheese

1 small lemon, cut into 8 wedges

1. Press the Sauté button on the Instant Pot® and heat oil. Add onion and cook until tender, about 3 minutes. Add garlic and cook until fragrant, about 30 seconds. Press the Cancel button.

2. Add beans, thyme, bay leaf, and water to the Instant Pot®. Close lid, set steam release to Sealing, press the Manual button, and set time to 50 minutes. When the timer beeps, quick-release the pressure until the float valve drops.

Open lid and check that beans are soft. If they are not tender, close lid and cook under pressure for 10 minutes more.

3. Add diced tomatoes and tomato sauce. Close lid and let stand on the Keep Warm setting for 10 minutes to heat through. Remove and discard bay leaf. Stir in herbs and ladle into soup bowls. Garnish with feta and lemon slices, and serve hot.

Per Serving

Calories: 241 | fat: 6g | protein: 14g | carbs: 33g | fiber: 10g | sodium: 458mg

89. Amaranth Salad

Prep time: 5 minutes | Cook time: 6 minutes | Serves 4

500ml water

192g amaranth

1g dried Greek oregano

3g salt

3g ground black pepper

15ml extra-virgin olive oil

10ml red wine vinegar

1. Add water and amaranth to the Instant Pot®. Close lid, set steam release to Sealing, press the Manual button, and set time to 6 minutes. When the timer beeps, quick-release the pressure until the float valve drops.
2. Open lid and fluff amaranth with a fork. Add oregano, salt, and pepper. Mix well. Drizzle with olive oil and wine vinegar. Serve hot.

Per Serving

Calories: 93 | fat: 5g | protein: 3g | carbs: 12g | fiber: 3g | sodium: 299mg

90. Puréed Red Lentil Soup

Prep time: 15 minutes | Cook time: 21 minutes | Serves 6

30ml olive oil

1 medium yellow onion, peeled and chopped

1 medium carrot, peeled and chopped

1 medium red bell pepper, seeded and chopped

1 clove garlic, peeled and minced

1 bay leaf

3g ground black pepper

1.5g salt

1 (425g) can diced tomatoes, drained

250g dried red lentils, rinsed and drained

1500ml low-sodium chicken stock

1. Press the Sauté button on the Instant Pot® and heat oil. Add onion, carrot, and bell pepper. Cook until just tender, about 5 minutes. Add garlic, bay leaf, black pepper, and salt, and cook until fragrant, about 30 seconds. Press the Cancel button.

2. Add tomatoes, lentils, and broth, then close lid, set steam release to Sealing, press the Manual button, and set time to 15 minutes. When the timer beeps, let pressure release naturally, about 15 minutes. Open lid, remove and discard bay leaf, and purée with an immersion blender or in batches in a blender. Serve warm.

Per Serving

Calories: 289 | fat: 6g | protein: 18g | carbs: 39g | fiber: 8g | sodium: 438mg

91. Lentil Pâté

Prep time: 10 minutes | Cook time: 34 minutes | Serves 12

30ml olive oil, divided

125g diced yellow onion

3 cloves garlic, peeled and minced

5ml red wine vinegar

250g dried green lentils, rinsed and drained

1000ml water

6g salt

1g ground black pepper

1. Press the Sauté button on the Instant Pot® and heat 15ml oil. Add onion and cook until translucent, about 3 minutes. Add garlic and vinegar, and cook for 30 seconds. Add lentils, water, remaining 15ml oil, and salt to pot and stir to combine. Press the Cancel button.

2. Close lid, set steam release to Sealing, press the Bean button, and allow to cook for default time of 30 minutes. When the timer beeps, let pressure release naturally for 10 minutes. Quick-release any remaining pressure until the float valve drops, then open lid.

3. Transfer lentil mixture to a food processor or blender, and blend until smooth. Season with pepper and serve warm.

Per Serving

Calories: 138 | fat: 3g | protein: 8g | carbs: 20g | fiber: 10g | sodium: 196mg

92. White Beans with Garlic and Tomatoes

Prep time: 10 minutes | Cook time: 40 minutes | Serves 6

125g dried cannellini beans, soaked overnight and drained

1000ml water

1000ml vegetable stock

15ml olive oil

6g salt

2 cloves garlic, peeled and minced

0.3g dried sage

3g ground black pepper

1. Add beans and water to the Instant Pot®. Close lid, set steam release to Sealing, press the Bean button, and cook for default time of 30 minutes. When timer beeps, quick-release the pressure until the float valve drops.
2. Press the Cancel button, open lid, drain and rinse beans, and return to pot along with stock. Soak for 1 hour.
3. Add olive oil, salt, garlic, tomato, sage, and pepper to beans. Close lid, set steam release to Sealing, press the Manual button, and set time to 10 minutes. When the timer beeps, quick-release the pressure until the float valve drops and open lid. Serve hot.

Per Serving

Calories: 128 | fat: 2g | protein: 7g | carbs: 20g | fiber: 4g | sodium: 809mg

93. Mediterranean "Fried" Rice

Prep time: 15 minutes | Cook time: 3 to 5 hours | Serves 4

Nonstick cooking spray

125g raw long-grain brown rice, rinsed

625ml low-sodium chicken stock

30ml extra-virgin olive oil

30ml balsamic vinegar

2 courgettes, diced

113g mushrooms, diced

1 small onion, diced

2 garlic cloves, minced

1 carrot, diced

1 bell pepper, any color, seeded and diced

31g peas (raw, frozen, or canned)

6g sea salt

454g boneless, skinless chicken breast, cut into ½-inch pieces

2 large eggs

1. Generously coat a slow-cooker insert with cooking spray. Put the rice, chicken broth, olive oil, vinegar, zucchini, mushrooms, onion, garlic, carrot, bell pepper, peas, and salt in a slow cooker. Stir to mix well.
2. Nestle the chicken into the rice mixture.
3. Cover the cooker and cook for 3 to 5 hours on Low heat.
4. In a small bowl, whisk the eggs. Pour the eggs over the chicken and rice. Replace the cover on the cooker and cook for 15 to 30 minutes on Low heat, or until the eggs are scrambled and cooked through.
5. Fluff the rice with a fork before serving.

Per Serving

Calories: 431 | fat: 14g | protein: 35g | carbs: 48g | fiber: 5g | sodium: 876mg

94. Creamy Thyme Polenta

Prep time: 5 minutes | Cook time: 10 minutes | Serves 6

875ml water

62g coarse polenta

62g fine cornmeal

125g corn kernels

1g dried thyme

6g salt

1. Add all ingredients to the Instant Pot® and stir.

2. Close lid, set steam release to Sealing, press the Manual button, and set time to 10 minutes. When the timer beeps, quick-release the pressure until the float valve drops and open lid. Serve immediately.

Per Serving

Calories: 74 | fat: 1g | protein: 2g | carbs: 14g | fiber: 2g | sodium: 401mg

95. Greek Yogurt Corn Bread

Prep time: 15 minutes | Cook time: 25 minutes | Serves 4 to 6

83ml olive oil, plus extra for greasing

125g cornmeal

125g plain flour

31g sugar

3g bicarbonate of soda

3g baking powder

5g sea salt

250g plain full-fat Greek yogurt

1 large egg

62g crumbled feta cheese

1. Preheat the oven to 375°F(190°C). Lightly grease an 8-inch square baking dish with olive oil.

2. In a large bowl, stir together the cornmeal, flour, sugar, baking soda, baking powder, and salt until well mixed. Add the yogurt, olive oil, and egg and stir until smooth. Stir in the feta.

3. Pour the batter into the prepared baking dish and bake until a toothpick inserted into the center of the corn bread comes out clean, about 30 minutes. 4. Remove the corn bread from the oven, cut it into 9 squares, and serve.

Per Serving

Calories: 546 | fat: 24g | protein: 11g | carbs: 71g | fiber: 2g | sodium: 584mg

Chapter 9 Vegetables and Sides

96. Spicy Grilled Veggie Pita

Prep time: 10 minutes | Cook time: 15 minutes | Serves 4

4 pita breads

30ml olive oil

2 garlic cloves, minced

1 courgette, sliced

1 red bell pepper, cut into strips

½ red onion, sliced

125g plain full-fat Greek yogurt

6g harissa

1 large tomato, sliced

3g Sea salt

2g Freshly ground black pepper

1. Toast the pitas in a skillet over medium-high heat for 3 to 4 minutes per side, then remove from the heat and set aside.
2. In the same skillet, combine the olive oil and garlic and sauté over medium-high heat for 2 minutes. Add the zucchini, bell pepper, and onion and sauté for 5 to 6 minutes, until softened. Remove from the heat.
3. While the vegetables are cooking, in a small bowl, mix the yogurt and harissa.
4. Halve the pitas crosswise and open each half to form a pocket. Add 18g the yogurt mixture to each pita pocket and spread it over the inside. Spoon the cooked vegetable mixture into the pockets and top with the tomatoes. Season with salt and black pepper.
5. Serve the pitas with the extra sauce on the side.

Per Serving

Calories: 215 | fat: 10g | protein: 5g | carbs: 27g | fiber: 5g | sodium: 244mg

97. Baba Ghanoush

Prep time: 15 minutes | Cook time: 2 to 4 hours | Serves 6

1 large aubergine (907 g to 1.8 kg), peeled and diced

62ml freshly squeezed lemon juice

2 garlic cloves, minced

30g tahini

15ml extra-virgin olive oil, plus more as needed

2g sea salt, plus more as needed

0.3g freshly ground black pepper, plus more as needed

8g chopped fresh parsley

1. In a slow cooker, combine the eggplant, lemon juice, garlic, tahini, olive oil, salt, and pepper. Stir to mix well.
2. Cover the cooker and cook for 2 to 4 hours on Low heat.
3. Using a spoon or potato masher, mash the mixture. If you prefer a smoother texture, transfer it to a food processor and blend to your desired consistency. Taste and season with olive oil, salt, and pepper as needed.
4. Garnish with fresh parsley for serving.

Per Serving

Calories: 81 | fat: 4g | protein: 3g | carbs: 12g | fiber: 4g | sodium: 108mg

98.Artichoke & Olive Dip

Prep time: 5 minutes | Cook time:10 minutes | Serves 6

1 x 400g can of chickpeas, drained and rinsed

4 artichoke hearts, drained and chopped

6 sun-dried tomatoes, finely chopped

30ml olive oil

Juice of 1 lemon

Salt and freshly ground black pepper

Toasted pitta bread or crudités, to serve

1.Place the chickpeas, artichoke hearts, sun-dried tomatoes, olive oil and lemon juice in a food processor or blender and blitz until smooth.
2.Season to taste with salt and pepper then transfer to a serving bowl.
3.Serve with toasted pitta bread or crudités.

Per Serving

Calories: 187 | fat: 11.5g | protein: 3.6g | carbs: 18.1g | fiber: 4.4g | sodium: 327mg

99. Vibrant Green Beans

Prep time: 10 minutes | Cook time: 15 minutes | Serves 6

30ml olive oil

2 leeks, white parts only, sliced

3g Sea salt and 0.5g freshly ground pepper, to taste

454g fresh green string beans, trimmed

5g Italian seasoning

30ml white wine

Zest of 1 lemon

1. Heat the olive oil over medium heat in a large skillet.
2. Add leeks and cook, stirring often, until they start to brown and become lightly caramelized.
3. Season with sea salt and freshly ground pepper.
4. Add green beans and Italian seasoning, cooking for a few minutes until beans are tender but still crisp to the bite.
5. Add the wine and continue cooking until beans are done to your liking and leeks are crispy and browned.
6. Sprinkle with lemon zest before serving.

Per Serving

Calories: 87 | fat: 5g | protein: 2g | carbs: 11g | fiber: 3g | sodium: 114mg

100. Couscous-Stuffed Eggplants

Prep time: 10 minutes | Cook time: 45 minutes | Serves 4

2 medium aubergines (about 227 g each)

15ml olive oil

42g whole-wheat couscous

45g diced dried apricots

4 spring onions, thinly sliced

1 large tomato, seeded and diced

6g chopped fresh mint leaves

15g chopped, toasted pine nuts

15ml lemon juice

3g salt

0.5g freshly ground black pepper

1. Preheat the oven to 400°F (205°C).

2. Halve the eggplants lengthwise and score the cut sides with a knife, cutting all the way through the flesh but being careful not to cut through the skin. Brush the cut sides with the olive oil and place the eggplant halves, cut-side up, on a large, rimmed baking sheet. Roast in the preheated oven for about 20 to 30 minutes, until the flesh is softened.

3. While the eggplant is roasting, place the couscous in a small saucepan or heat-safe bowl and cover with boiling water. Cover and let stand until the couscous is tender and has absorbed the water, about 10 minutes.

4. When the eggplants are soft, remove them from the oven (don't turn the oven off) and scoop the flesh into a large bowl, leaving a bit of eggplant inside the skin so that the skin holds its shape. Be cautious not to break the skin. Chop or mash the eggplant flesh and add the couscous, dried apricots, scallions, tomato, mint, pine nuts, lemon juice, salt, and pepper and stir to mix well.

5. Spoon the couscous mixture into the eggplant skins and return them to the baking sheet. Bake in the oven for another 15 minutes or so, until heated through. Serve hot.

Per Serving

Calories: 146 | fat: 5g | protein: 4g | carbs: 22g | fiber: 6g | sodium: 471mg

101. Spina ch and Sweet Pepper Poppers

Prep time: 10 minutes | Cook time: 8 minutes | Makes 16 poppers

113g cream cheese, softened

125g chopped fresh spinach leaves

3g garlic powder

8 mini sweet bell peppers, tops removed, seeded, and halved lengthwise

1. In a medium bowl, mix cream cheese, spinach, and garlic powder. Place 15g mixture into each sweet pepper half and press down to smooth.

2. Place poppers into ungreased air fryer basket. Adjust the temperature to 400°F (204°C) and air fry for 8 minutes. Poppers will be done when cheese is browned on top and peppers are tender-crisp. Serve warm.

Per Serving

Calories: 31 | fat: 2g | protein: 1g | carbs: 3g | fiber: 0g | sodium: 34mg

102. Braised Eggplant and Tomatoes

Prep time: 10 minutes | Cook time: 40 minutes | Serves 4

1 large aubergine, peeled and diced

Pinch sea salt

1 (425g) can chopped tomatoes and juices

250ml chicken stock

2 garlic cloves, smashed

5g Italian seasoning

1 bay leaf

Pinch sea salt and freshly ground pepper, to taste

1. Cut the eggplant, and salt both sides to remove bitter juices. Let the eggplant sit for 20 minutes before rinsing and patting dry.
Dice eggplant.
3. Put eggplant, tomatoes, chicken broth, garlic, seasoning, and bay leaf in a large saucepot.
4. Bring to a boil and reduce heat to simmer.
5. Cover and simmer for about 30–40 minutes until eggplant is tender. Remove garlic cloves and bay leaf, season to taste, and serve.

Per Serving

Calories: 70 | fat: 1g | protein: 4g | carbs: 14g | fiber: 6g | sodium: 186mg

103. Glazed Carrots

Prep time: 10 minutes | Cook time: 8 to 10 minutes | Serves 4

10g honey

15ml orange juice

8g grated orange rind

0.5g ginger

454g baby carrots

30ml olive oil

1.5g salt

1. Combine honey, orange juice, grated rind, and ginger in a small bowl and set aside.
2. Toss the carrots, oil, and salt together to coat well and pour them into the air fryer basket.

3. Roast at 390°F (199°C) for 5 minutes. Shake basket to stir a little and cook for 2 to 4 minutes more, until carrots are barely tender.
4. Pour carrots into a baking pan.
5. Stir the honey mixture to combine well, pour glaze over carrots, and stir to coat.
6. Roast at 360°F (182°C) for 1 minute or just until heated through.

Per Serving

Calories: 71 | fat: 2g | protein: 1g | carbs: 12g | fiber: 3g | sodium: 234mg

104. Sesame Carrots and Sugar Snap Peas

Prep time: 10 minutes | Cook time: 16 minutes | Serves 4

454g carrots, peeled sliced on the bias (½-inch slices)

5ml olive oil

3g Salt and 0.5g freshly ground black pepper, to taste

42g honey

15ml sesame oil

15ml soy sauce

3g minced fresh ginger

113g sugar snap peas

5g sesame seeds

1. Preheat the air fryer to 360°F (182°C).
2. Toss the carrots with the olive oil, season with salt and pepper and air fry for 10 minutes, shaking the basket once or twice during the cooking process
3. Combine the honey, sesame oil, soy sauce and minced ginger in a large bowl. Add the sugar snap peas and the air-fried carrots to the honey mixture, toss to coat and return everything to the air fryer basket.
4. Turn up the temperature to 400°F (204°C) and air fry for an additional 6 minutes, shaking the basket once during the cooking process.
5. Transfer the carrots and sugar snap peas to a serving bowl. Pour the sauce from the bottom of the cooker over the vegetables and sprinkle sesame seeds over top. Serve immediately.

Per Serving

Calories: 202 | fat: 6g | protein: 2g | carbs: 37g | fiber: 4g | sodium: 141mg

105. Sautéed Fava Beans with Olive Oil, Garlic, and Chiles

Prep time: 10 minutes | Cook time: 7 minutes | Serves 4

1.6kg fresh broad beans, shelled

30ml olive oil

2 cloves garlic, minced

10ml fresh lemon juice

5g finely grated lemon zest

3g crushed red pepper flakes

3g salt

0.5g freshly ground black pepper

1. Bring a medium saucepan of lightly salted water to a boil. Add the shelled favas and cook for 3 to 4 minutes, until tender. Drain the favas and immediately place them in an ice water bath to stop their cooking. When cool, peel the tough outer skin off the beans.
2. Heat the olive oil in a large skillet over medium-high heat. Add the garlic and cook, stirring, until it is aromatic but not browned, about 30 seconds. Add the beans and cook, stirring, until heated through, about 2 minutes. Stir in the lemon juice, lemon zest, red pepper flakes, salt, and pepper and remove from the heat. Serve immediately.

Per Serving

Calories: 576 | fat: 9g | protein: 39g | carbs: 88g | fiber: 38g | sodium: 311mg

106. Roasted Cauliflower and Tomatoes

Prep time: 5 minutes | Cook time: 25 minutes | Serves 4

500g cauliflower, cut into 1-inch pieces

90ml extra-virgin olive oil, divided

6g salt, divided

500g cherry tomatoes

1g freshly ground black pepper

125g grated Parmesan cheese

1. Preheat the oven to 425°F(220°C).
2. Add the cauliflower, 45ml olive oil, and 3g salt to a large bowl and toss to evenly coat. Pour onto a baking sheet and spread the cauliflower out in an even

layer.

3.In another large bowl, add the tomatoes, remaining 45ml olive oil, and 3g salt, and toss to coat evenly. Pour onto a different baking sheet.

4.Put the sheet of cauliflower and the sheet of tomatoes in the oven to roast for 17 to 20 minutes until the cauliflower is lightly browned and tomatoes are plump.

5. Using a spatula, spoon the cauliflower into a serving dish, and top with tomatoes, black pepper, and Parmesan cheese. Serve warm.

Per Serving

Calories: 294 | fat: 26g | protein: 9g | carbs: 13g | fiber: 4g | sodium: 858mg

107. Parmesan-Thyme Butternut Squash

Prep time: 15 minutes | Cook time: 20 minutes | Serves 4

313g butternut squash, cubed into 1-inch pieces (approximately 1 medium)

30ml olive oil

1.5g salt

1g garlic powder

0.5g black pepper

1g fresh thyme

60g grated Parmesan

1. Preheat the air fryer to 360°F(182°C).
2. In a large bowl, combine the cubed squash with the olive oil, salt, garlic powder, pepper, and thyme until the squash is well coated.
3. Pour this mixture into the air fryer basket, and roast for 10 minutes. Stir and roast another 8 to 10 minutes more.
4. Remove the squash from the air fryer and toss with freshly grated Parmesan before serving.

Per Serving

Calories: 127 | fat: 9g | protein: 3g | carbs: 12g | fiber: 2g | sodium: 262mg

108 Lightened-Up Eggplant Parmigiana

Prep time: 10 minutes | Cook time: 1 hour 20 minutes | Serves 3

2 medium globe aubergines, sliced into ¼-inch rounds

30mlextra virgin olive oil, divided

6g fine sea salt, divided

1 medium onion (any variety), diced

1 garlic clove, finely chopped

567g canned crushed tomatoes or tomato purée

3g chopped fresh basil, divided

0.5g freshly ground black pepper

198g low-moisture mozzarella, thinly sliced or grated

57g grated Parmesan cheese

1. Line an oven rack with aluminum foil and preheat the oven to 350°F (180°C).
2. Place the eggplant slices in a large bowl and toss with 15ml the olive oil and 3g the sea salt. Arrange the slices on the prepared oven rack. Place the oven rack in the middle position and roast the eggplant for 15–20 minutes or until soft.
3. While the eggplant slices are roasting, heat 15ml the olive oil in a medium pan over medium heat. When the oil begins to shimmer, add the onions and sauté for 5 minutes, then add the garlic and sauté for 1 more minute. Add the crushed tomatoes, 1.5g of the basil, 3g the sea salt, and 0.5g black pepper. Reduce the heat to low and simmer for 15 minutes, then remove from the heat.
4. When the eggplant slices are done roasting, remove them from the oven. Begin assembling the dish by spreading 125g the tomato sauce over the bottom of a 11 × 7-inch (30 × 20cm) casserole dish. Place a third of the eggplant rounds in a single layer in the dish, overlapping them slightly, if needed. Layer half of the mozzarella on top of the eggplant, then spread 188g tomato sauce over the cheese slices and then sprinkle 625g the grated Parmesan cheese over the top. Repeat the process with a second layer of eggplant, sauce, and cheese, then add the remaining eggplant in a single layer on top of the cheese. Top with the remaining sauce and then sprinkle the remaining 1.5g basil over the top.
5. Bake for 40–45 minutes or until browned, then remove from oven and set aside to cool for 10 minutes before cutting into 6 equal-size pieces and serving. Store covered in the refrigerator for up to 3 days.

Per Serving

Calories: 453 | fat: 28g | protein: 28g | carbs: 26g | fiber: 4g | sodium: 842mg

109. Greek Fasolakia (Green Beans)

Prep time: 10 minutes | Cook time: 6 to 8 hours | Serves 6

907g green beans, trimmed
1 (425g) can no-salt-added diced tomatoes, with juice
1 large onion, chopped
4 garlic cloves, chopped
Juice of 1 lemon
1g dried dill
3g ground cumin
1g dried oregano
6g sea salt
1g freshly ground black pepper
62g feta cheese, crumbled

1.In a slow cooker, combine the green beans, tomatoes and their juice, onion, garlic, lemon juice, dill, cumin, oregano, salt, and pepper. Stir to mix well.
2.Cover the cooker and cook for 6 to 8 hours on Low heat.
3. Top with feta cheese for serving.

Per Serving

Calories: 94 | fat: 2g | protein: 5g | carbs: 18g | fiber: 7g | sodium: 497mg

Chapter 10 Staples, Sauces, Dips, and Dressings

110. Berry and Honey Compote

Prep time: 5 minutes | Cook time: 15 minutes | Serves 2 to 3

62g honey

31g fresh berries

30g grated orange zest

1. In a small saucepan, heat the honey, berries, and orange zest over medium-low heat for 2 to 5 minutes, until the sauce thickens, or heat for 15 seconds in the microwave. Serve the compote drizzled over pancakes, muffins, or French toast.

Per Serving

Calories: 272 | fat: 0g | protein: 1g | carbs: 74g | fiber: 1g | sodium: 4mg

111. Orange Dijon Dressing

Prep time: 5 minutes | Cook time: 0 minutes | Serves 2

62ml extra-virgin olive oil

30ml freshly squeezed orange juice

1 orange, zested

5g garlic powder

2g za'atar seasoning

3g salt

1g Dijon mustard

0.5g Freshly ground black pepper, to taste

1. In a jar, combine the olive oil, orange juice and zest, garlic powder, za'atar, salt, and mustard. Season with pepper and shake vigorously until completely mixed.

Per Serving

Calories: 284 | fat: 27g | protein: 1g | carbs: 11g | fiber: 2g | sodium: 590mg

112. Classic Basil Pesto

Prep time: 5 minutes | Cook time: 13 minutes | Makes about 378g

6 garlic cloves, unpeeled

62g pine nuts

80g fresh basil leaves

16g fresh parsley leaves

250ml extra-virgin olive oil

28g Parmesan cheese, grated fine

1. Toast garlic in 8-inch skillet over medium heat, shaking skillet occasionally, until softened and spotty brown, about 8 minutes. When garlic is cool enough to handle, remove and discard skins and chop coarsely. Meanwhile, toast pine nuts in now-empty skillet over medium heat, stirring often, until golden and fragrant, 4 to 5 minutes.

2. Place basil and parsley in 1-gallon zipper-lock bag. Pound bag with flat side of meat pounder or with rolling pin until all leaves are bruised.

3. Process garlic, pine nuts, and herbs in food processor until finely chopped, about 1 minute, scraping down sides of bowl as needed. With processor running, slowly add oil until incorporated. Transfer pesto to bowl, stir in Parmesan, and season with salt and pepper to taste. (Pesto can be refrigerated for up to 3 days or frozen for up to 3 months. To prevent browning, press

plastic wrap flush to surface or top with thin layer of olive oil. Bring to room temperature before using.)

Per Serving(63g)

Calories: 423 | fat: 45g | protein: 4g | carbs: 4g | fiber: 1g | sodium: 89mg

113. Citrus Vinaigrette

Prep time: 2 minutes | Cook time: 0 minutes | Serves 4

Zest of 1 lemon

45ml fresh lemon juice

Pinch coarse sea salt

Pinch freshly ground black pepper

30ml olive oil

1. In a small bowl, whisk together the lemon zest, lemon juice, 45ml water, the salt, and the pepper. While whisking, gradually stream in the olive oil and whisk until emulsified. Store in an airtight container in the refrigerator for up to 3 days.

Per Serving

Calories: 65 | fat: 7g | protein: 0g | carbs: 2g | fiber: 0g | sodium: 146mg

114. White Bean Hummus

Prep time: 10 minutes | Cook time: 30 minutes | Serves 12

94g dried white beans, rinsed and drained

3 cloves garlic, peeled and crushed

62ml olive oil

115ml lemon juice

3g salt

1. Place beans and garlic in the Instant Pot® and stir well. Add enough cold water to cover ingredients. Close lid, set steam release to Sealing, press the Manual button, and set time to 30 minutes.
2. When the timer beeps, let pressure release naturally, about 20 minutes. Press the Cancel button and open lid. Use a fork to check that beans are tender. Drain off excess water and transfer beans to a food processor.
3. Add oil, lemon juice, and salt to the processor and pulse until mixture is

smooth with some small chunks. Transfer to a storage container and refrigerate for at least 4 hours. Serve cold or at room temperature. Store in the refrigerator for up to one week.

Per Serving

Calories: 57 | fat: 5g | protein: 1g | carbs: 3g | fiber: 1g | sodium: 99mg

115. Sweet Red Wine Vinaigrette

Prep time: 5 minutes | Cook time: 0 minutes | Serves 2

92ml extra-virgin olive oil

30ml red wine vinegar

15ml apple cider vinegar

10g honey

10g Dijon mustard

3g minced garlic

1g coarse sea salt

0.3g freshly ground black pepper

1. In a jar, combine the olive oil, vinegars, honey, mustard, garlic, salt, and pepper and shake well.

Per Serving

Calories: 386 | fat: 41g | protein: 0g | carbs: 6g | fiber: 0g | sodium: 198mg

116. Maltese Sun-Dried Tomato and Mushroom Dressing

Prep time: 10 minutes | Cook time: 5 minutes | Serves 4

83ml olive oil (use a combination of olive oil and sun-dried tomato oil, if they were packed in oil)

227g mushrooms, sliced

45ml red wine vinegar

1g Freshly ground black pepper, to taste

62g sun-dried tomatoes, drained (if they are packed in oil, reserve the oil) and chopped

1. In a medium skillet, heat 30ml the olive oil (or mixed olive oil and sun-dried tomato packing oil) over high heat. Add the mushrooms and cook, stirring, until they have released their liquid.

2. Add vinegar and season with pepper. Remove from the heat and add the remaining oil and the sun-dried tomatoes.

Per Serving(250g)

Calories: 190 | fat: 18g | protein: 3g | carbs: 6g | fiber: 2g | sodium: 21mg

117. Vinaigrette

Prep time: 5 minutes | Cook time: 0 minutes | Serves 4

30ml balsamic vinegar

2 large garlic cloves, minced

1g dried rosemary, crushed

1g freshly ground black pepper

62ml olive oil

1. In a small bowl, whisk together the vinegar, garlic, rosemary, and pepper. While whisking, slowly stream in the olive oil and whisk until emulsified. Store in an airtight container in the refrigerator for up to 3 days.

Per Serving(250ml)

Calories: 129 | fat: 1g | protein: 3g | carbs: 0g | fiber: 0g | sodium: 2mg

118. Tabil (Tunisian Five-Spice Blend)

Prep time: 2 minutes | Cook time: 0 minutes | Makes 6g Tabil

3g ground coriander

2g caraway seeds

1g garlic powder

0.5g cayenne pepper

0.6g ground cumin

1. Combine all the ingredients in a small bowl.

2. It may be stored in an airtight container for up to 2 weeks.

Per Serving

Calories: 13 | fat: 1g | protein: 1g | carbs: 2g | fiber: 1g | sodium: 2mg

119. Cider Yogurt Dressing

Prep time: 5 minutes | Cook time: 0 minutes | Serves 2

250g plain, unsweetened, full-fat Greek yogurt

125ml extra-virgin olive oil

15ml apple cider vinegar

½ lemon, juiced

3g chopped fresh oregano

1g dried parsley

3g coarse sea salt

1g garlic powder

0.6g freshly ground black pepper

1. In a large bowl, combine the yogurt, olive oil, vinegar, lemon juice, oregano, parsley, salt, garlic powder, and pepper and whisk well.

Per Serving

Calories: 402 | fat: 40g | protein: 8g | carbs: 4g | fiber: 1g | sodium: 417mg

120. Apple Cider Dressing

Prep time: 5 minutes | Cook time: 0 minutes | Serves 2

30ml apple cider vinegar

⅓ lemon, juiced

⅓ lemon, zested

Pinch salt and freshly ground black pepper, to taste

1. In a jar, combine the vinegar, lemon juice, and zest. Season with salt and pepper, cover, and shake well.

Per Serving

Calories: 7 | fat: 0g | protein: 0g | carbs: 1g | fiber: 0g | sodium: 1mg

121. Olive Tapenade

Prep time: 10 minutes | Cook time: 0 minutes | Makes about 250g

94g pitted brine-cured green or black olives, chopped fine

1 small shallot, minced

30ml extra-virgin olive oil

15g capers, rinsed and minced

8ml red wine vinegar

1g minced fresh oregano

1. Combine all ingredients in bowl. (Tapenade can be refrigerated for up to 1 week.)

Per Serving(63g)

Calories: 92 | fat: 9g | protein: 0g | carbs: 2g | fiber: 1g | sodium: 236mg

122. Riced Cauliflower

Prep time: 5 minutes | Cook time: 10 minutes | Serves 6 to 8

1 small head cauliflower, broken into florets
62ml extra-virgin olive oil
2 garlic cloves, finely minced
9g salt
1g freshly ground black pepper

1. Place the florets in a food processor and pulse several times, until the cauliflower is the consistency of rice or couscous.
2. In a large skillet, heat the olive oil over medium-high heat. Add the cauliflower, garlic, salt, and pepper and sauté for 5 minutes, just to take the crunch out but not enough to let the cauliflower become soggy.
3. Remove the cauliflower from the skillet and place in a bowl until ready to use. Toss with chopped herbs and additional olive oil for a simple side, top with sautéed veggies and protein, or use in your favorite recipe.

Per Serving

Calories: 69 | fat: 7g | protein: 1g | carbs: 2g | fiber: 1g | sodium: 446mg

Appendix 1 Measurement Conversion Chart

MEASUREMENT CONVERSION CHART

VOLUME EQUIVALENTS (DRY)

US STANDARD	METRIC (APPROXIMATE)
1/8 teaspoon	0.5 mL
1/4 teaspoon	1 mL
1/2 teaspoon	2 mL
3/4 teaspoon	4 mL
1 teaspoon	5 mL
1 tablespoon	15 mL
1/4 cup	59 mL
1/2 cup	118 mL
3/4 cup	177 mL
1 cup	235 mL
2 cups	475 mL
3 cups	700 mL
4 cups	1 L

VOLUME EQUIVALENTS (LIQUID)

US STANDARD	US STANDARD (OUNCES)	METRIC (APPROXIMATE)
2 tablespoons	1 fl.oz.	30 mL
1/4 cup	2 fl.oz.	60 mL
1/2 cup	4 fl.oz.	120 mL
1 cup	8 fl.oz.	240 mL
1 1/2 cup	12 fl.oz.	355 mL
2 cups or 1 pint	16 fl.oz.	475 mL
4 cups or 1 quart	32 fl.oz.	1 L
1 gallon	128 fl.oz.	4 L

TEMPERATURES EQUIVALENTS

FAHRENHEIT(F)	CELSIUS(C) (APPROXIMATE)
225 °F	107 °C
250 °F	120 °C
275 °F	135 °C
300 °F	150 °C
325 °F	160 °C
350 °F	180 °C
375 °F	190 °C
400 °F	205 °C
425 °F	220 °C
450 °F	235 °C
475 °F	245 °C
500 °F	260 °C

WEIGHT EQUIVALENTS

US STANDARD	METRIC (APPROXIMATE)
1 ounce	28 g
2 ounces	57 g
5 ounces	142 g
10 ounces	284 g
15 ounces	425 g
16 ounces (1 pound)	455 g
1.5 pounds	680 g
2 pounds	907 g

Appendix 2 Measurement Conversion Chart

The Dirty Dozen and Clean Fifteen

The Environmental Working Group (EWG) is a nonprofit, nonpartisan organization dedicated to protecting human health and the environment Its mission is to empower people to live healthier lives in a healthier environment. This organization publishes an annual list of the twelve kinds of produce, in sequence, that have the highest amount of pesticide residue-the Dirty Dozen-as well as a list of the fifteen kinds ofproduce that have the least amount of pesticide residue-the Clean Fifteen.

THE DIRTY DOZEN

- The 2016 Dirty Dozen includes the following produce. These are considered among the year's most important produce to buy organic:

Strawberries	Spinach
Apples	Tomatoes
Nectarines	Bell peppers
Peaches	Cherry tomatoes
Celery	Cucumbers
Grapes	Kale/collard greens
Cherries	Hot peppers

- The Dirty Dozen list contains two additional itemskale/collard greens and hot peppers-because they tend to contain trace levels of highly hazardous pesticides.

THE CLEAN FIFTEEN

- The least critical to buy organically are the Clean Fifteen list. The following are on the 2016 list:

Avocados	Papayas
Corn	Kiw
Pineapples	Eggplant
Cabbage	Honeydew
Sweet peas	Grapefruit
Onions	Cantaloupe
Asparagus	Cauliflower
Mangos	

- Some of the sweet corn sold in the United States are made from genetically engineered (GE) seedstock. Buy organic varieties of these crops to avoid GE produce.

Printed in Great Britain
by Amazon